P9-DCP-778

THE AMERICAN BAR ASSOCIATION

GUIDE TO MARRIAGE, DIVORCE & FAMILIES

THE AMERICAN BAR ASSOCIATION

Guide to Marriage, Divorce & Families

RANDOM HOUSE REFERENCE
NEW YORK   TORONTO   LONDON   SYDNEY   AUCKLAND

Copyright © 2006 by the American Bar Association

All rights reserved. Published in the United States by Random House Reference, an imprint of The Random House Information Group, a division of Random House, Inc., New York, and simultaneously in Canada by Random House of Canada Limited, Toronto. No part of this book may be reproduced in any form or by any means, electronic or mechanical, including photocopying, recording, or by any information storage and retrieval system, without the written permission of the publisher. All inquiries should be addressed to Random House Reference, Random House Information Group, 1745 Broadway, New York, NY 10019.

RANDOM HOUSE is a registered trademark of Random House, Inc.

Please address inquiries about electronic licensing of reference products for use on a network, in software, or on CD-ROM to the Subsidiary Rights Department, Random House Reference, FAX 212-572-6003.

This book is available at special discounts for bulk purchases for sales promotions or premiums. Special editions, including personalized covers, excerpts of existing books, and corporate imprints, can be created in large quantities for special needs. For more information, write to Random House, Inc., Special Markets/Premium Sales, 1745 Broadway, MD 6-2, New York, NY, 10019 or e-mail *specialmarkets@randomhouse.com*.

Visit the Random House Reference Web site: *www.randomwords.com*

Library of Congress Cataloging-in-Publication Data is available.
The American Bar Association guide to marriage, divorce & families.
    p.   cm.
ISBN-10: 0-375-72138-X (alk. paper)
ISBN-13: 978-0-375-72138-0
1. Domestic relations—United States. I. Title: Guide to marriage, divorce & families. II. American Bar Association.
KF505.A87 2006
346.7301'5—dc22   2005055098
            0 9 8 7 6 5 4 3 2 1

ISBN-13: 978-0-375-72138-0

ISBN-10: 0-375-72138-X

AMERICAN BAR ASSOCIATION

Robert A. Stein
Executive Director

Sarina A. Butler
Associate Executive Director, Communications Group

Mabel C. McKinney-Browning
Director, Division for Public Education

Charles White
Katherine Fraser
Series Editors

Jeff Atkinson
Principal Author
Adjunct Professor
DePaul University College of Law, Chicago, Illinois

REVIEWERS

Barbara Atwood
James E. Rogers College of Law
University of Arizona,
Tucson, Arizona

Lynne Gold-Bikin
Past-Chair, ABA Family
Law Section
Norristown, Pennsylvania

Linda Elrod
Director, Washburn Law School
Children and Family Center
Editor-in-Chief, ABA *Family
Law Quarterly*
Topeka, Kansas

Honorable James A. Knecht
Justice of the Appellate Court
Fourth District
Bloomington, Illinois

Honorable Jerelyn D. Maher
Judge of the Circuit Court
Tenth Judicial Circuit
Tremont, Illinois

James H. Feldman
Jenner & Block LLP
Chicago, Illinois

Donald C. Schiller
Schiller, Du Canto and Fleck
Chicago, Illinois

Ronald W. Nelson
Nelson & Booth
Overland Park, Kansas

Carolyn J. Stevens
Stevens Law Office
Lolo, Montana

Harlan Tenenbaum
Chair, ABA Committee
on Adoption
Wilmington, Delaware

Alan S. Kopit
Chair
Hahn Loeser & Parks LLP
Cleveland, Ohio

Harry S. Johnson
Maryland State Bar Association
Baltimore, Maryland

David Anderson
U.S. Court of Appeals for the
Armed Forces
Dunn Loring, Virginia

Honorable Linda McGee
North Carolina Court
of Appeals
Raleigh, NC

Daniel O'Neil Bernstine
President, Portland State
University
Portland, Oregon

Gary Slaiman
Swidler & Berlin
Washington, DC

David A. Collins
General Motors Legal Staff
Detroit, Michigan

Dwight L. Smith
Attorney at Law
Tulsa, Oklahoma

Jeffrey J. Snell
Attorney at Law
Sagamore Hills, Ohio

Okianer Christian Dark
Professor of Law
Howard University School of Law
Washington, D.C.

W. Scott Welch
Butler Snow O'Mara Stevens
et. al.
Jackson, Mississippi

James Dimos
Locke Reynolds LLP
Indianapolis, Indiana

David Williams
Vanderbilt University
Nashville, Tennessee

Juanita C. Hernandez
Ogletree Deakins
San Antonio, Texas

CONTENTS

FOREWORD
FROM THE ABA

Robert A. Stein, *Executive Director,*
American Bar Association

When American families are asked to describe their legal needs, the topics that come up repeatedly are housing, personal finance, wills and estates, employment-related issues, and family and domestic concerns, usually in conjunction with divorce and child support. The books in the *American Bar Association Legal Guide* series are designed to address these key legal areas, and provide information about the law in plain, direct language.

The goal of the series is to help you make informed decisions on how best to handle your own particular questions by providing information on the range of options that can be used in solving everyday legal problems. We hope that these books will help you feel more comfortable with the law and will take much of the mystery out of the legal system.

As the largest voluntary association in the world and the nation's premier source of legal information, the American Bar Association is in a unique position to provide authoritative guidance on legal issues. The ABA also provides support for lawyer referral programs and pro bono services (where lawyers donate their time), so that finding the right lawyer and receiving quality legal help within your budget is an attainable goal.

This book was written with the aid of ABA members—including lawyers, judges, and academics—from across the country. Their contribution is valuable because they have experience in dealing with family law issues every day; their perspectives and expertise make this a better book. The ABA's Standing Committee on Public Education provided oversight for this project. The programs, publications, and resources of the ABA Division for Public Education are designed to educate the public about the rule of law, and ensure that people understand and participate in our legal system. Public education and public service are two of the most important goals of the American Bar Association. Through publications, outreach, and our website (www. abanet.org), the ABA continues to provide accurate, unbiased legal information to our members, to the media, and to the general public.

Robert A. Stein is the executive director of the American Bar Association. He was formerly dean of the University of Minnesota Law School.

PREFACE

Alan S. Kopit, *Chair*
ABA Standing Committee on Public Education

The U.S. Census Bureau reported in 2003 that while 57.3 million American households included a married couple, Americans are waiting until later in life to marry and are postponing the decision to have children. Moreover, married couples are more likely to divorce than in the past, and there are more households than ever that do not fit into the traditional mold.

In 2003, the Census Bureau reported there were 4.6 million households consisting of an unmarried man and an unmarried woman living together. In addition, there were 659,000 of what the Census Bureau calls "unmarried-partner households": 333,000 comprised of two male partners, and 326,000 comprised of two female partners. The law can affect children, finances, health care choices, and property in all of these families.

If you say, "I do," you make a personal and a legal commitment to another person. What you may not realize is that you also obtain a battery of legal rights and responsibilities with your marriage certificate. Many of the rights and responsibilities accorded automatically to married couples will only be relevant if you subsequently divorce or separate. For example, marriage entitles a person to an equitable distribution of marital property upon divorce. Marriage also entitles a person to seek financial support in the event of a separation or divorce. If you are unmarried and living with your partner, you are not automatically entitled to many of the rights that married people enjoy, and you must act to secure and protect your rights.

Whether you're married, divorced, or living with your partner, you need this book. It gives you the complete run-down on your rights and responsibilities under the law with respect to spouses, partners and children. It gives you pointers on how to take the maximum advantage of legal protections. It gives you information about when you might need a lawyer. And it brings you up to date on the latest changes in family law and how they can affect you.

NEW AND IMPROVED EDITION

This book is a complete revision and update of an earlier book in the ABA Legal Guide Series. We've taken into account all the changes in the law, and added a new chapter on same-sex marriages, civil unions, and domestic partnerships. Our principal author also wrote the first edition of this book, entitled the *American Bar Association Guide to Family Law*. Jeff Atkinson is a law professor and writer who has written widely in the area. His manuscript was reviewed and approved by experts on family law from across the country, with particular assistance from the ABA's Family Law Section. We've worked to provide you with easy-to-read information that will help you understand and use the law that affects you and your family.

WRITTEN WITH YOU IN MIND

We've made a special effort to make this book practical, by using situations and problems you are likely to encounter. You won't find legal jargon or technicalities here—just concise, straightforward discussions of your options under the law. Each chapter opens with a description of a real-life problem that shows the practical ramifications of the subject. Within chapters, you'll find sidebars with the following icons:

- ▶, which share practical tips that could be of benefit to you;
- ⓘ, which signal key additional information, including information on important court cases;
- ⚠, which warn you about potential pitfalls that you can navigate with the right information and help;

- ▤ , which give clear, plain English definitions to legal terms;
- 〈〉 , which highlight experts' responses to practical questions, giving legal information that may help you as you grapple with similar issues within your own family.

You'll find two additional features at the end of each chapter:

- "The World at Your Fingertips," which contains tips on where to go for more information if you'd like to explore a topic further.
- "Remember This," which highlights the most important points that the chapter has covered.

One word of caution: when reading this book, and other books in the series, keep in mind that these books cannot and do not pretend to provide legal advice. Only a lawyer who understands the facts of your particular case can do that. Although every effort has been made to present material that is as up-to-date as possible, laws can and do change. Laws can also vary widely from one jurisdiction to the next. If you are thinking about pursuing legal action, you should consult first with a lawyer, bar association, or lawyer referral service.

With that in mind, this book will help you make informed decisions about a wide range of problems and opportunities. Armed with the knowledge and insights this book provides, you can be confident that the decisions you make will be in your best interests.

Alan S. Kopit is a legal-affairs commentator who has appeared on national television for more than fifteen years. He is chair of the ABA's Standing Committee on Public Education and is an attorney in private practice with the firm of Hahn Loeser & Parks, LLP, in Cleveland, Ohio.

INTRODUCTION

Family law has been evolving for about as long as human beings have been evolving. Even when people lived together in tribes without formal governments, they developed their own customs or adopted rules from their deities.

In Western culture, particularly after the Norman Conquest in 1066, regulation of marriage and divorce was placed initially in the hands of the church. As church and state grew more separate, however, civil courts and legislatures took over more of the regulation of family law. And that's when things started to get complicated.

Some may wish for a simpler time—when a man and woman could be married simply by exchanging promises to one another, without the need for paperwork or outside officials. In other cultures and times, even divorce was simpler: A Pueblo woman could divorce her husband simply by placing his moccasins outside their door, and a Muslim man could divorce his wife simply by pronouncing the *Talaq* ("I divorce thee; I divorce thee; I divorce thee").

But as our society has become more advanced, the rules of family law have become more complicated—even with periodic legislative reforms to simplify the rules. The goal of this book is to explain these rules, with the hope of making this often-confusing area of law seem less daunting.

Special attention is given to the laws of divorce—particularly the factors judges consider when deciding issues of property, alimony, child support, custody, and allocation of time with children. In addition, this book addresses other issues of family law, such as the requirements that must be met before getting married, rights of persons living together, prenuptial agreements, procedures for adoption, and domestic violence.

Family law, also known as "matrimonial law" or the "law of domestic relations," often involves a great deal of stress. When people need information about family law, it is usually because they are experiencing—or contemplating—significant changes in their lives, such as divorce or separation. Even those issues of family law associated with happier events, such as marriage or adoption, can bring their share of stresses.

Knowledge of the law does not eliminate all the anxieties that may accompany a legal issue, but it is a step in the right direction. Much of the tension that people feel during a legal dispute comes from not knowing their options, or from not knowing what to expect. This book will provide you with a greater understanding of the rights and responsibilities of people who are married, divorced, or living together. In addition, the information in this book will prepare you to work with others, including your attorney, to resolve disputes and plan for the future.

As noted periodically throughout this book, laws vary from state to state, and courts within a state may even decide a particular issue in different ways. For specific analysis of your state's law, you should consult an attorney in your state who is experienced in family law.

Jeff Atkinson
Author
Member, ABA Family Law Section

CHAPTER 1
Premarital Agreements

Elizabeth and Joe, both thirty-eight, plan to marry. Elizabeth owns and is the president of her own company, which has profits of more than $5 million per year. Joe, a consultant, has an income of $110,000 per year. Elizabeth would like to have a premarital agreement to protect her interest in her company and her income. What are the criteria for a valid premarital agreement?

A premarital agreement—also referred to as an **antenuptial agreement**—is a contract entered into by two people before they marry. The agreement usually describes what each party's rights will be if they divorce or if one of them dies. Premarital agreements most commonly deal with issues of property and support—for example, describing the property and support, if any, to which each party will be entitled in the event of divorce or death.

REASONS FOR PREMARITAL AGREEMENTS

People intending to marry use premarital agreements for several reasons, some of which may be interrelated. First and foremost, premarital agreements help to clarify the parties' expectations and rights for the future. Specifically, such agreements may prevent a couple from developing uncertainties and fears about how a divorce court might divide property and decide spousal support if the marriage fails.

In addition, a person who wants a future spouse to sign a premarital agreement often has something he or she wants to protect—usually money. One or both partners may want to avoid the risk of a major loss of assets, income, or a family business in the event of divorce.

People marrying for a second or third time also might wish to ensure that, in the event of their death, certain assets or personal belongings are passed on to the children or grandchildren of prior marriages rather than to a current spouse.

By signing a premarital agreement, the less-wealthy spouse generally is giving something up. Specifically, he or she is agreeing to have his or her property rights determined by the agreement rather than by the usual rules of law that a court would apply in the event of divorce or death. As will be discussed later (see chapter 10), courts have rules for dividing property when a couple divorces. In some states, such as California, courts automatically divide the property acquired by a husband and wife during their marriage equally. In most states, courts divide property in a way that the court deems fair, and the result is less predictable. The split is not necessarily fifty-fifty.

If a spouse dies, courts normally follow the instructions of his or her will. But state laws dictate that the surviving spouse usually is entitled to one-third or one-half of the estate, regardless of the will's instructions. If the husband and wife have signed a valid premarital agreement, however, that agreement will supersede the usual laws governing division of property and income upon death. In many cases, the less-wealthy spouse will receive less under the premarital agreement than he or she would have received under the usual laws governing divorce or wills.

If a less-wealthy spouse will receive less under a premarital agreement than under the general laws governing divorce and death, why would he or she choose to sign such an agreement? The answer to that question depends on the individual.

Some people prefer to control their fiscal relationships rather than leave them to state regulation. They may want to avoid uncertainty about what courts might decide if their marriages end in divorce. For some, the answer may be that "love conquers all"—in other words, the less-wealthy person may simply want to marry the other person, and may not care much about the financial details. For others, a premarital agreement may provide ample security, even if such an agreement might not prove as generous as a judge when it comes to division of assets. Still others may not like the idea of a premarital agreement, but are willing to take their chances and hope their relationship and financial arrangements will work out for the best.

CRITERIA FOR A VALID AGREEMENT

The laws governing the validity of premarital agreements vary from state to state. In general, however, such agreements must be in writing and signed by both parties.

Most states require that parties to a premarital agreement disclose their income and assets to one another. However, sometimes it is difficult to determine precisely a party's net worth. For example, if one spouse owns a business that is **closely held**— meaning that shares of the company's stock are not traded on a public stock market—it may be difficult to ascertain the value of the business. In such a circumstance, it usually is best to acknowledge the difficulty of precise valuation in the agreement, and then state the minimum net worth or the range of possible net worths for the party in question.

In order to be valid, a premarital agreement must not be the result of **fraud** or **duress.** An agreement is the result of fraud if, for example, one party—particularly the wealthier

 TELL ALL!

In most states, the parties to a premarital agreement—particularly the wealthier party—must disclose their income and assets to one another. This way, each person will know more about what he or she might be giving up. In some states, it may be possible to waive one's right to full disclosure of income and assets, but the person waiving that right should do so knowingly—and it is best if each party has at least a general idea of the other's net worth.

one—deliberately misstates his or her financial condition. Thus, if a man hides assets from his future wife so that she will agree to a lower level of support in the event of divorce, a court would likely declare the resulting agreement invalid. Similarly, if one person exerts excessive emotional pressure on the other to sign an agreement, a court would likely declare that agreement invalid on the grounds of duress.

An agreement might be valid even if both parties were not represented by lawyers, but using lawyers is still a good idea in order to ensure that the agreement is drafted properly and that both parties are making informed decisions.

The lawyer for the wealthier party usually prepares the initial draft of the agreement. The less-wealthy party and his or her attorney, if any, should review the agreement carefully and ask questions about any matters that are uncertain. The likelihood of producing a valid, enforceable agreement increases if the less-wealthy party's interests are well represented and if some back-and-forth negotiations take place.

In order to demonstrate that the parties truly understand the terms to which they are agreeing, some attorneys also favor tak-

 AVOIDING DURESS

In order to avoid the appearance of duress and to give the parties ample time to consider their agreement, a premarital agreement should be reviewed and signed well before the wedding. Most states do not specify a "cutoff" time by which premarital agreements must be signed, but the longer the parties have to consider an agreement, the greater the likelihood that a court will deem it voluntary.

If the wealthier party presents an agreement to his or her prospective spouse for the first time too close to the wedding—say, the day before—a court may later find the agreement invalid on grounds of duress. A last-minute premarital agreement will not automatically be deemed invalid, but timing may nonetheless be a significant factor in the eyes of a court.

WHEN AN AGREEMENT IS ENFORCEABLE

Mary and John are in their late forties. They plan to marry in five months. Each has been married before. Before getting married, however, they wish to clarify their financial relationship. Mary has assets of about $400,000; John has assets of about $200,000. They both work and are capable of self-support. They each wish to protect the assets that they will bring into the marriage.

After disclosing their assets to each other and consulting with their individual attorneys, Mary and John sign an agreement that provides:

- Each spouse's future earnings will remain his or her separate property, as long as such earnings are kept in accounts bearing only the name of the person who earned them;

- The savings, investments, and retirement accounts that each spouse brings into the marriage, along with any growth in those assets, will remain his or her separate property after the marriage, as long as such assets are held only in that spouse's name;

- Each party waives any right to future alimony or inheritance, although either party is free to include the other in his or her will;

- The parties, if they wish, may make joint investments, such as in a house, condominium, or car, in which case title will be held jointly with a **right of survivorship**—which means that if one of them dies, the other will receive the property that was jointly held; and

- The parties will share common expenses, including housing, utilities, and food, in proportion to their incomes.

Since the agreement appears to be fair and not made under duress, a court would likely deem it valid and enforceable.

ing certain additional steps. For example, in addition to signing the agreement, the parties might place their initials on pages with key provisions, such as those pertaining to disclosures of assets, distribution of property, and support. The parties—particularly the less-wealthy party—might also be asked to prepare handwritten statements, in their own words, reflecting their understanding of and consent to the agreement. Alternatively, the signing of the agreement might be videotaped or audiotaped, with the parties providing oral statements of their understanding and consent to the agreement in addition to their written consent.

AMOUNT OF SUPPORT

State laws do not specify an amount of support that must be provided by premarital agreements. Thus, after a divorce, if two parties are capable of self-support based on their assets, income, and job skills, a court could uphold an agreement that provided no property or support to the less-wealthy spouse.

However, if the less-wealthy spouse cannot be financially self-sufficient, and the agreement provides him or her with little or no property or support, courts in most states would likely step in and order some distribution of property or support in his or her favor. The amount of such a distribution will vary from state to state. In some states, the amount need only enable a subsistence level of living on the part of the less-wealthy spouse— enough to keep him or her off the welfare roles—while other courts may apply broader notions of fairness and require a higher level of support.

A standard used by some courts is **unconscionability**. The term refers to agreements that are unusually harsh or unfair; an unconscionable agreement is one that no sensible person would offer and no sensible person—that is, no person not under duress or delusion—would accept. Because the standard is subjective, courts have interpreted the term "unconscionability" in different ways. But the bottom line is that if a court finds an agreement to be unconscionable, the agreement will not be enforced.

Under a law called the Uniform Premarital Agreement Act (UPAA), adopted by approximately half the states, unconscionability alone does not render an agreement unenforceable. Under the UPAA, the party seeking to have an agreement held unenforceable on the basis of unconscionability also must show three things: (1) that he or she was not "provided a fair and reasonable disclosure of the property or financial obligations of the other party"; (2) that he or she did not waive such disclosure in writing; and (3) that he or she "did not have, or reasonably could not have had, an adequate knowledge of the property or financial obligations of the other party."

Nonetheless, under the UPAA, a court may order support if the elimination or modification of support under a premarital agreement will result in "undue hardship in light of circumstances not reasonably foreseen" at the time the agreement was signed. For example, if a young working woman signed a premarital agreement that left her with no support in the event of divorce, and then suffered a disabling injury after fifteen years of marriage, a court probably would order support in the event of her divorce.

For a discussion of general standards for dividing property and alimony or maintenance in the absence of a valid premarital agreement, see chapters 10 and 11.

If the wealthier spouse is concerned that the value of his or her assets could decrease sharply at a later time, he or she may

ESCALATOR CLAUSES

To promote fairness and avoid unconscionability, many lawyers drafting premarital agreements favor inclusion of an **escalator clause** or a **phase-in provision** that will increase the amount of assets or support given to the less-wealthy spouse based on the length of the marriage or an increase in the wealthier party's assets or income after the agreement is made.

wish to include a provision that provides protection in such a circumstance. For example, if a premarital agreement provides for a fixed dollar amount to the less-wealthy spouse, the wealthier party might add a provision stating that in no event shall the amount of property given to the other spouse exceed, say, half of the wealthier party's assets. Alternatively, the amount of assets to be paid in the event of divorce or death could be calculated as a percentage of the wealthier party's assets at that time.

NON-BINDING ISSUES

Although premarital agreements can be binding on issues of property division and alimony, they are not binding on issues of child custody or child support. Parties cannot make arrangements before they marry regarding the custody of a child in the event of divorce. Courts remain the ultimate guardians of children's best interests—and, as such, do not want to encourage husbands and wives to bargain away what is best for their children. Thus, while a court may consider what a couple declared to be best for their children in a premarital agreement, it will not be bound by that agreement in making its decision.

Premarital agreements regarding child support are not binding on courts for similar reasons. If such an agreement exists and meets a child's reasonable needs, a court may choose to follow it, but is not required to do so. (This is also the case with agreements regarding the division of household chores.) For a description of applicable standards regarding child custody and child support, see Chapters 12 and 13.

RELATED DOCUMENTS

When future spouses sign a premarital agreement, they may also sign related documents to help carry out their wishes. For example, one partner to the marriage may sign an agreement creating a **trust**. A trust is a legal device by which the title to property is held by one party for the benefit of another party. For example, money in a bank account, shares of stock in a company, or deeds to land may all be placed in a trust. A **trustee** will have the power to manage the property in the trust for benefit of the person for whom the trust was created—the **beneficiary.** You may wish to create a trust even if you are unmarried.

A trust created in connection with a premarital agreement might be used to manage and protect the assets of the wealthier party. A trust also might be used to establish a fund for the benefit of the less-wealthy party. For example, in a premarital agreement, the wealthier party may agree to place a certain amount of money each year into a trust for the benefit of the less-wealthy party. Deposits would continue to be made for the length of the marriage, perhaps up to a maximum number of years or a maxi-

---

 TALKING TO A LAWYER

Q. I am sixty-two years old and getting married for the second time. I want to be able to leave most of my money to my adult children, my grandchildren, and a charity with which I have worked. I also want to provide financial security to my new spouse, although my spouse has money too. How do I handle this?

A. A premarital agreement would be helpful. Without a premarital agreement, a surviving spouse can challenge your will and claim a portion of your estate—often as much as one-third to one-half of the estate, depending on the state in which you live. Another option is to set up a trust to provide funds for your children, grandchildren, charities, and surviving spouse. A lawyer can advise you of more specific options and the requirements for each of these approaches. In any case, you and your spouse should discuss the proposed premarital agreement or estate planning and try to devise an approach with which you are both comfortable.

Answer by Professor Jeff Atkinson,
DePaul University College of Law, Chicago, Illinois

mum dollar amount. In the event of divorce or death, the less-wealthy party's entitlement to assets might be limited to whatever is in the trust.

Another agreement that might be signed at the same time as a premarital agreement is a **contract to make a will,** under which the parties agree in advance to the terms of their wills. For example, the parties may wish to agree that children from prior marriages—or from their own marriage—will receive specified amounts of their estates.

Contracts to make a will have the advantage of clarifying the parties' rights and responsibilities, but have the disadvantage of lessening the parties' flexibility. If circumstances change, a party who has signed a contract to make a will may not be able to change his or her will without the other party's consent. If, for instance, one party wishes to include a new person or charity in his or her will, he or she may no longer be able to do so, depending on how the contract was written.

POSTMARITAL AGREEMENTS

Postmarital agreements or **postnuptial agreements** are agreements entered into after a marriage has taken place, but before the parties seek to end their marriage. As with premarital agreements, one or both of the parties usually is seeking to protect assets or income in the event of divorce or death. A married couple may seek to enter into a postmarital agreement after a significant financial change or a period of marital conflict.

The law regarding the validity and enforcement of postmarital agreements is not well developed. The standard for enforcement of such agreements most likely is similar to the standards discussed earlier for enforcement of premarital agreements. Key criteria for validity of the agreements include: full disclosure of assets and financial obligations, absence of duress, and fairness.

When two people are married, as opposed simply to contemplating marriage, they may be held to a very high standard of

CLARITY AND FAIRNESS

When entering into a postmarital agreement, it is a good idea for the parties to articulate in writing why they are entering into the agreement and to ensure that the agreement is fair for both parties.

fairness with respect to financial issues—perhaps an even higher standard than if they were entering into a premarital agreement.

THE WORLD AT YOUR FINGERTIPS

- Additional information about prenuptial agreements can be obtained in a question-and-answer format from the "Free Advice" website at *http://family-law.freeadvice.com*. Click on "Premarital Agreement" at the top of the page.
- A description of each state's laws regarding premarital agreements is available at FindLaw: *http://public.findlaw.com/family/*. This site also features frequently asked questions about such agreements.
- The Equality in Marriage Institute provides general information on how people can protect themselves and their finances when they enter into marriage. Information on prenuptial agreements and other issues to consider before marriage is available at *www.equalityinmarriage.org/bm.html*.

REMEMBER THIS

Prenuptial agreements are generally legal. In order to ensure validity, it is important that the parties

- disclose their assets and income to each other, or explicitly waive full disclosure;
- clearly understand the agreement and what each person is giving up; and

- have sufficient time to consider the agreement and are not under duress when the agreement is signed.

Having lawyers represent each party is not absolutely essential, but representation of each party makes it more likely that each person's needs will be met and that the agreement will be valid.

CHAPTER 2
Valid and Invalid Marriages

George and Sally have lived together for fifteen years, and have two children. They have told neighbors they are married, and have filed joint tax returns, but have never obtained a marriage license or participated in a marriage ceremony. Does the law consider them married? Is this a common-law marriage?

Most states define marriage as a civil contract between a man and woman to become husband and wife.

The moment a woman and man marry, their relationship acquires legal status. As the United States Supreme Court said of marriage in an 1888 case, "[t]he relation once formed, the law steps in and holds the parties to various obligations and liabilities."

The rights and obligations of married persons are not the same as those of single persons. Married persons may have rights to their partners' property and future incomes; they may have rights to certain benefits, including family health insurance and survivor's benefits; they may be responsible for each other's debts; and they are subject to different tax rates than single persons. State and federal laws, as well as an employer's policies, determine the scope of a married person's new rights and duties. After all, marriage is a private bond between two people, but it is also an important social institution.

As our society changes, there is no longer a short answer to the question "What is marriage?" Definitions of and opinions about the proper functions of marriage continue to differ. The women's rights movement and the lesbian, gay, bisexual, and transgender (LGBT) movements have changed some people's ideas of marriage—a fact that reminds us that marriage will remain, but will continue to evolve. (Chapter 3 will discuss marriage between persons of the same sex, domestic partnerships, and related issues.)

REQUIREMENTS FOR GETTING MARRIED

The requirements that a couple must meet in order to get married are simple, though they vary from state to state. In general, a man and woman wishing to marry must obtain a license in the state where they wish to be married, usually from a county clerk or a clerk of court. Usually, the fee for obtaining such a license is low.

Before issuing a license, many states require the man and woman to undergo blood tests to screen them for venereal disease—though generally not for AIDS. Some states do not require this test if the couple in question has already been living together. If a blood test indicates that a would-be spouse is the carrier of a venereal disease, certain states will not issue a license. Other states will allow the marriage as long as the couple knows the disease is present.

In some states, the couple must show proof of immunity or vaccination for certain diseases in order to obtain a marriage license. A few states also demand a general physical examination.

If one or both of the parties has been married before, all states require that the earlier marriage have ended as the result of death, divorce, or annulment—though in some states, if a marriage was never valid, a legal action for annulment may not be necessary.

In addition, parties who wish to marry must have the **capacity** to do so. In other words, the man and woman must understand that they are being married and what it means to be married. If one of the parties lacks capacity because of drunkenness, mental illness, or some other problem, the marriage will not be valid.

Close blood relatives cannot marry, although in some states, first cousins can marry. Of the states that allow first cousins to marry, a few also require that one of the cousins no longer be able to conceive children.

Most, but not all, states require a waiting period after the license is issued—generally one to five days. The purpose of the waiting period is to allow a brief "cooling-off" period during which the parties can change their minds if they wish to do so. However, the waiting period generally can be waived for good reason. For example, if the groom is arriving in the bride's town only one day before the wedding, but the state has a three-day waiting period, the waiting period probably could be waived by a judge or clerk of court.

In almost all states, a man or woman may marry at age eighteen without parental consent. Most states also allow persons age sixteen and seventeen to marry, with the consent of either their parents or a judge.

Finally, a marriage that is valid in the state or country where it was performed generally will be considered valid in a state or country to which the couple later moves, unless the marriage is deemed to violate a fundamental policy of that state. For example, same-sex marriage would violate the public policy of some states, so a marriage performed in one state might not be recognized in another. Other examples of marriages that might violate a fundamental policy of a state and therefore be invalid include a polygamous marriage (entered into in a country that allowed such marriages) or marriages of close relatives.

THE MARRIAGE CEREMONY

A marriage ceremony may be religious or civil. A religious ceremony is typically conducted in accordance with the religious customs of the bride or groom—or, in the case of a Native American group, in accordance with the customs of the applicable tribe. Religious ceremonies normally are conducted by religious officials, such as ministers, priests, or rabbis, while Native American ceremonies may be presided over by a tribal chief or other designated official.

THE PROCESS OF GETTING MARRIED

Civil ceremonies usually are conducted by judges. In some states, county clerks or other government officials also may conduct civil ceremonies. Contrary to popular legend, however, no state authorizes ship captains to perform marriages.

Most states require one or two witnesses to sign a marriage certificate. The person who performs a marriage ceremony must send a copy of the marriage certificate to the county or state agency responsible for recording marriage certificates. Failure to send the marriage certificate to the appropriate agency does not necessarily nullify the marriage, but it may make proof of the marriage more difficult.

States generally do not require that certain words be used in a marriage ceremony, but the person or persons conducting the ceremony should indicate that the man and woman agree to be married.

Most states consider a couple to be married when the ceremony ends. Lack of subsequent sexual relations does not automatically affect the validity of the marriage, though in some states nonconsummation could constitute grounds for annulment. (For more information on annulments, see Chapter 9.)

COMMON-LAW MARRIAGES

In times past, particularly in frontier days, it was common for states to consider a woman and man married if they lived together for a certain length of time, had sexual intercourse, and represented themselves to others as husband and wife, even if they never held a marriage ceremony. Such a marriage was often called a **common-law marriage.**

Today, approximately three-quarters of the states no longer recognize common-law marriages. The remaining states recognize common-law marriages, but with significant restrictions. Specifically, in the states that continue to recognize common-law marriages, such marriages require that a man and woman: have the capacity to marry; regard themselves as husband and wife; live together; and clearly represent themselves to others as husband and wife. A man and woman may represent themselves as husband and wife through their words to others, by filling out joint tax returns, or by completing other forms that identify them as married. Merely living together is not enough to create a common-law marriage.

If a common-law marriage is valid, the partners have the same rights and duties as they would if they were parties to a ceremonial marriage. An interesting problem arises if a couple with

 STATES THAT RECOGNIZE COMMON-LAW MARRIAGE

Alabama

Colorado

Georgia (if the relationship existed before January 1, 1997)

Idaho (if the relationship existed before January 1, 1996)

Iowa

Kansas

Montana

New Hampshire (for inheritance purposes only)

Ohio (if the relationship existed before October 10, 1991)

Oklahoma

Pennsylvania (if the relationship existed before January 1, 2005)

Rhode Island

South Carolina

Texas

Utah

Washington, D.C.

CHANGE OF NAME

A woman who marries may change her last name—also known as her "surname"—to that of her husband, but she is not required to do so. In the past, it was widely assumed that a woman would change her last name to her husband's name when she married. Today, society recognizes a woman's right to take her husband's name, keep her original name, or use both names. The general rule is that if a woman uses a certain name consistently and honestly, then that is her true name.

a valid common-law marriage in one state moves to a state that does not recognize such marriages: Is the marriage still valid? According to **conflict of laws** principles, the answer is usually "yes." Such principles generally state that if a contract—in this case, a marriage agreement—is valid in the state where it is created, it will be treated as valid in any other state to which its parties move, even if those parties could not have entered into such an agreement in the new state.

Parties to a valid common-law marriage can only end the marriage, for legal purposes, with a formal divorce. There is no United States counterpart to the Muslim tradition that allows divorce to be accomplished simply by the husband pronouncing the *Talaq:* "I divorce thee; I divorce thee; I divorce thee;"

INVALID MARRIAGES

Occasionally, people who live as a married couple learn that their marriage is not legal. For example, one supposed spouse may have kept a prior marriage secret, or both may have thought incorrectly that an earlier marriage had ended in divorce or the death of a spouse. In addition, a marriage may be invalid because it took place between close relatives, underage persons, or people incapable of entering into a marriage contract because of mental incompetence.

If a marriage is invalid for any of the reasons listed above, a court may grant an **annulment** instead of a divorce. An annulment is a legal declaration that a valid marriage never existed—as opposed to a divorce, which is a legal declaration that such a marriage existed but is now over. (For additional discussion of divorces, see Chapter 9.)

When a court grants an annulment, the parties often are free to go their separate ways without any further legal obligations to each other. Many states, however, apply additional principles of

 TALKING TO A LAWYER

Q. *After a night of drinking, a man and woman decide to fly to Las Vegas, obtain a marriage license, and get married in a wedding chapel by "Elvis." Two days later, they have second thoughts about the marriage. Is the marriage valid?*

A. One would need a few more facts to determine whether the marriage is valid. A valid marriage requires that the parties have the capacity to marry—including the mental ability to know that they were entering into a marriage. Although the man and woman had been drinking, they seem to have been competent enough to arrange for a flight to Las Vegas, obtain a wedding license, and stand up and say they wanted to be married. Given these facts, the marriage most likely would be deemed valid—assuming all other legal requirements for marriage were met—which means that if the parties wanted to end their marriage, they would need to obtain a divorce. If one or both parties were so intoxicated that they did not know what was going on, then the marriage would not be valid, and the parties probably could obtain an annulment instead of a divorce.

Answer by Professor Jeff Atkinson,
DePaul University College of Law, Chicago, Illinois

law to protect persons who believe themselves to be in valid marriages when they, in fact, are not. An individual who wrongly believes that he or she is in a valid marriage is referred to as the **putative spouse,** and the rule of law that protects that person is sometimes referred to as the **putative-spouse doctrine**—though in many states the remedy may be known by other names.

Under the putative-spouse doctrine, a putative spouse may be entitled to the same benefits and rights as a legal spouse for as long as she or he reasonably believes a marriage to be valid. From time to time, people discover that their marriage is invalid only when filing for divorce. In such a situation, after a long union that both parties believed to be valid, a court may refuse to declare the union an invalid marriage. Instead, it may deem the marriage valid and require a divorce in order to end it. In such an event, the usual rules of property distribution and support apply, and an economically dependent spouse may be able to obtain more property and support than he or she would have obtained had the marriage been annulled. (The rules of property distribution and alimony will be discussed further in later chapters.)

If one party to a marriage believes it to be valid, but the other party knows differently, an additional principle may apply: **estoppel**. Estoppel is a legal principle that prevents a person, because of his or her prior conduct, from doing something that he or she would otherwise be entitled to do. In legal language, a person may be **estopped** from acting in a certain way as a result of his or her past actions. In this case, if one party to a marriage tricks the other into thinking the marriage is valid, a court might estop the deceiver—that is, prevent him or her—from later claiming the marriage to be invalid. Thus, the deceiving partner would not be able to profit from property division or support settlements that resulted from the deception.

If one party to a marriage learns of such a deception and then promptly seeks to annul the marriage—as opposed to seeking a divorce—a court likely would grant the annulment. On the other hand, if the deceived party learned of the deception and nonetheless chose to remain in the marriage for a long period of time before seeking to end it, the doctrine of **laches**—that is, long delay—may prevent even the "innocent" party from successfully seeking to declare the marriage invalid. In such a case, the parties may be required to follow the rules of divorce rather than annulment.

THE WORLD AT YOUR FINGERTIPS

• A chart detailing the requirements for getting married—including age of consent, waiting periods, and medical exams—can be obtained from the Legal Information Institute of Cornell University at *www.law.cornell.edu/topics/Table_Marriage.htm*.

• Further information on laws regarding marriage, wedding planning, and traveling abroad to get married is available at *http://usmarriagelaws.com*.

REMEMBER THIS

• Marriage is governed by laws in each state.

• The age at which people can marry without parental consent is generally eighteen.

• Some states require blood tests before issuing a marriage license.

• Most state laws no longer recognize common-law marriages formed within the state.

CHAPTER 3

Same-Sex Marriages, Civil Unions, and Domestic Partnerships

Tina and Megan have lived together in a committed relationship for three years. They would like to make their relationship more "official" and enjoy the same legal protections afforded to married couples. What are their options?

Same-sex partners may have several options if they wish to formalize their relationship. Depending on the state in which they live, they may be able to enter into a civil union, register as domestic partners or get married.

SAME-SEX MARRIAGE

In 2003, the Supreme Judicial Court of Massachusetts ruled in the case of *Goodridge v. Department of Public Health* that persons of the same sex have the same right to marry as persons of different sexes. In that case, seven same-sex couples in what the court described as "committed relationships" sought to obtain marriage licenses, but were unable to do so because state statutes did not recognize same-sex marriages.

The court in *Goodridge* held that limiting the right to civil marriage to different-sex couples violates principles of liberty and equality under the Massachusetts Constitution. It said that the prohibition of same-sex marriage, like the historical prohibition of interracial marriages, "deprives individuals of access to an institution of fundamental legal, personal, and social significance."

In response to arguments that only marriages between people of different sexes could provide a "favorable setting for procreation" and raising children, the court said that "[f]ertility is not a condition of marriage, nor is it grounds for divorce. . . . The 'best interests of the child' standard does not turn on a parent's sexual orientation or marital status." The court concluded:

> Certainly our decision today marks a significant change in the definition of marriage as it has been inherited from the common law, and understood by many societies for centuries. But it does not disturb the fundamental value of marriage in our society.

The court noted that under established principles of law, states are allowed to interpret state constitutions in ways that grant individuals broader rights than the U.S. Constitution.

Three justices on the *Goodridge* court dissented. All three argued that the decision whether to allow same-sex marriage should be made by the legislature, not the court. One justice said: "The power to regulate marriage lies with the Legislature, not with the judiciary. . . . Such a dramatic change in social institutions must remain at the behest of the people through the democratic process." He further argued that, before a court creates a new constitutional right of a fundamental nature, the asserted right must be "objectively, deeply rooted in this Nation's history and tradition"—which, he said, same-sex marriage is not.

CIVIL UNIONS

The state of Vermont also has granted broad rights to same-sex couples. In the 1999 case *Baker v. State,* the state supreme court held that Vermont's constitution requires the same benefits and protections for same-sex couples as it does for married couples. The court did not require that same-sex couples be allowed to marry, but it did require that the state legislature provide them with "the common benefits and protections that flow from marriage under Vermont law."

In response to the court's ruling, the Vermont legislature passed a statute establishing **civil unions,** which grant same-sex couples the same rights as married couples. The equal rights granted, however, exist only under the state law of Vermont. The

Vermont legislature and courts cannot control the application of federal laws to same-sex couples; thus, for example, federal laws regarding joint tax returns, Social Security survivors benefits, and immigration status for family members are not affected by Vermont's civil-union laws.

In 1993, the Hawaii Supreme Court held in *Baehr v. Lewin* that the state's prohibition of same-sex marriage appeared to be sex discrimination and a denial of equal protection under the state constitution. While the case was still pending, the Hawaii Constitution was amended to allow the legislature to preclude such marriages, and the legislature did so. The case was then dismissed as **moot**—meaning that a ruling would no longer be of practical significance, since the constitutional provision on which the original case was based had been changed.

Meanwhile, courts in at least seven other states have held that the denial of marriage rights to same-sex couples does not violate state or federal constitutions.

As of 2005, three countries recognize the right of same-sex couples to marry: Belgium, Canada, and the Netherlands. In addition, many other countries—including several in Europe—recognize partnerships or pacts granting most of the rights and responsibilities of marriage to same-sex couples.

DEFENSE OF MARRIAGE LAWS

In the mid-1990s, many states began enacting **defense of marriage acts,** also referred to as "**DOMAs**." The purpose of state DOMAs is to prohibit same-sex couples from marrying within the applicable states, and to provide that those states will refuse to recognize same-sex marriages performed in other states. By 2005, forty states had passed DOMAs.

Most of the initial DOMAs were parts of state statutes governing marriage. However, in the wake of decisions from state courts finding rights under state constitutions for same-sex couples to marry, some states passed amendments to their constitutions declaring that marriage can only legally exist between a

LEGAL ISSUES ARISING FROM SAME-SEX MARRIAGES

More than one thousand rights and responsibilities are automatically accorded to married couples. Institutions that recognize same-sex marriages must afford these same rights and responsibilities to same-sex married couples.

Same-sex couples can be granted rights and responsibilities by state governments, local governments, the federal government, private employers, and other private organizations. However, the fact that one unit of government—such as a state government—grants such recognition does not necessarily require other units of government or organizations to do the same.

What follows is a list of the rights that would be granted to same-sex couples in various key areas of state and federal law, if governments, employers, or private-sector organizations were to recognize same-sex marriages. (Keep in mind that these rights might also apply to civil unions and domestic partnerships, though the scope of the rights granted will vary depending on how the law is drafted.)

Family Law—right to distribution of property upon divorce; right to seek support (i.e., alimony); right to seek custody, visitation, or parenting time; right to adopt; right to care for a foster child

Taxation—right to file jointly and utilize married persons' tax rates

Health-Care Law—right to make decisions on behalf of an incapacitated partner; right to access medical records

Probate—right of intestate succession (i.e., right to inherit property when a partner dies without a will); protection from disinheritance; right to preferential status in the selection of a guardian or executor

Torts—rights to seek compensation for wrongful death and loss of consortium (i.e., companionship)

Government Benefits—right to survivor benefits, including Social Security; right to military benefits, including housing, commissary, survivor benefits, and education for children

Private-Sector Benefits—right to family health insurance; eligibility for life insurance; right to take sick leave to care for a family member; eligibility for family memberships

Real Estate—eligibility for tenancy by the entirety (a form of property ownership in which joint ownership and right of survivorship generally cannot be eliminated if one partner transfers his or her interest to another—traditionally available only to husbands and wives); homestead rights (which may protect a couple's home from forced sale for collection of debts, or may result in favorable property-tax treatment)

Bankruptcy—right to file jointly for bankruptcy; right to preferential treatment of spouse for claims made in a divorce decree or separation agreement, including **nondischargeability** of spousal support (i.e., refusal of the bankruptcy court to excuse payment of alimony debts—a form of protection for the spouse who is owed such payments)

Immigration—right to joint petitions for immigration; right to preferred status for spouses or family members immigrating separately

Criminal Law—privilege of refusing to testify; right to protections under domestic violence laws

man and a woman. By including DOMAs in state constitutions rather than crafting them as separate statutes, many states seek to prevent their courts from using state constitutions to extend marriage rights to same-sex couples.

The U.S. government also has created defense of marriage statutes. One such law declares that no state—or territory or Indian tribe—within the United States shall be required to recognize same-sex marriages performed in another state. Another law provides that, for the purpose of any federal law or regulation, "the word 'marriage' means only a legal union between one man and one woman as husband and wife."

In addition, Congress is considering an amendment to the U.S. Constitution that would similarly restrict the definition of "marriage." One draft of the proposed amendment provides: "Marriage in the United States shall consist only of the union of a man and a woman. Neither this Constitution, nor the constitution of any State, shall be construed to require that marriage or the legal incidents thereof be conferred upon any union other than the union of a man and a woman."

An amendment to the United States Constitution must be approved by a two-thirds vote of both the House and the Senate and by three-quarters of the states.

DOMESTIC PARTNERSHIPS

Some state and local governments allow persons of the same sex—and, in some jurisdictions, persons of different sexes—to

 STEPS DOMESTIC PARTNERS CAN TAKE FOR THEMSELVES

Regardless of whether two people who regard themselves as domestic partners live in a jurisdiction that officially recognizes domestic partnerships, there are certain things they can do to ensure themselves more rights and protections:

- Sign health-care powers of attorney granting each person the right to make health-care decisions for the other in the event of incapacity;
- Sign powers of attorney that allow each person to make financial decisions and manage property for the other in the event of incapacity;
- Hold property—such as a home, car, or financial accounts—in joint tenancy with rights of survivorship so that upon the death of one partner, the property will pass to the surviving partner;
- Write wills leaving property, including items of personal significance, to each other;
- Take out life insurance policies naming each other as beneficiaries; and
- Write and sign an agreement as to the sharing of expenses and property during the relationship.

register as domestic partners. The benefits and rights that arise from a domestic partnership vary from jurisdiction to jurisdiction. Common rights include: eligibility for family health insurance, the right to sick leave to care for a family member or partner, the right to bereavement leave, rights to visit a partner in the hospital, and the right to make health-care decisions for an incapacitated partner.

In addition to being recognized by many governmental units, domestic partnerships are also recognized by many private employers for the purpose of granting certain benefits, particularly eligibility for family health insurance and leave to take care of a sick family member or partner.

 TALKING TO A LAWYER

Q. Do civil unions and domestic partnerships offer the same rights and protections as marriage?

A. The extent to which civil unions and domestic partnerships provide the same protections as marriage depends on the wording of the applicable laws. In Vermont, the civil union law extends all of the rights and benefits of marriage to partners in a civil union, but the domestic partnership laws of many cities and counties in the United States provide only limited rights, such as hospital visitation privileges.

Answer by Professor Barbara Atwood, Mary Anne Richey Professor of Law, University of Arizona, Tucson, Arizona

Q. If a same-sex couple were to be married in Massachusetts, would the couple be considered married in another state?

A. Under the Full Faith and Credit Clause of the Constitution and the federal Defense of Marriage Act, states are not required to recognize a same-sex marriage performed in another state.

Answer by Professor Barbara Atwood, Mary Anne Richey Professor of Law, University of Arizona, Tucson, Arizona

THE WORLD AT YOUR FINGERTIPS

• You can find more information about the rights of same-sex couples, including state-by-state information and workplace issues, at the website of the Human Rights Campaign at *www.hrc.org*.

• The website of Lambda Legal provides fact sheets and backgrounders on the issue of same-sex marriage, as well as up-to-date information on the latest legal cases in this area, at *www. lambdalegal.org*.

• A summary of conservative and liberal views about same-sex marriages can be obtained from The American Voice at *www.americanvoice2004.org/samesexmarriage/#Anchor-The-49575*.

REMEMBER THIS

• The supreme courts of some states have declared that same-sex couples are entitled to marry, or at least to have the same rights as married couples of different sexes. In response, many states have passed statutes or constitutional amendments restricting the definition of "marriage" to include only the union between a man and woman.

• Many state and local governments and private employers recognize domestic partnerships. The benefits available to members of such partnerships vary, but often include the right to family health insurance and the right to take leave to care for a sick domestic partner.

• There are several steps that same-sex couples can take to ensure each partner more rights and protections—such as drafting powers of attorney, writing wills, and holding property in joint tenancy with right of survivorship.

CHAPTER 4
Living Together

Carol and Ray have been together for nine months and consider themselves to be in a committed relationship. They plan to rent an apartment together and share common expenses. Each of them would like the other to make health-care decisions in the event of his or her incapacity. What steps should they take to accomplish these goals?

The U.S. Census Bureau reports that in 2003, there were 4.6 million households consisting of an unmarried man and an unmarried woman living together. In addition, there were 659,000 of what the Census Bureau dubs "unmarried-partner households": 333,000 comprised of two male partners, and 326,000 comprised of two female partners. (The Census Bureau noted that these numbers may actually be higher than are listed in its report, since some people may be reluctant to label themselves "partners" on census forms.) By comparison, there were 58.6 million households comprised of wives and husbands living together.

LEGALITY OF LIVING TOGETHER

It is perfectly legal for an unmarried couple to live together; such couples generally can live wherever they wish. Some local zoning laws prohibit more than three unrelated persons from living together in one house or apartment, but such laws do not apply to two-person households. Although a few states do have criminal laws prohibiting cohabitation, such laws generally are not enforced. Moreover, a state government's attempt to prevent an adult couple from living together probably would be considered a violation of the couple's rights to free association and due process under the First and Fourteenth Amendments to the United States Constitution.

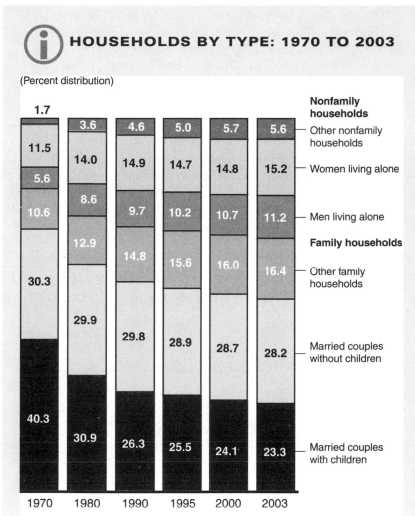

HOUSEHOLDS BY TYPE: 1970 TO 2003

(Percent distribution)

Nonfamily households

Other nonfamily households
Women living alone
Men living alone

Family households

Other family households
Married couples without children
Married couples with children

	1970	1980	1990	1995	2000	2003
Other nonfamily households	1.7	3.6	4.6	5.0	5.7	5.6
Women living alone	11.5	14.0	14.9	14.7	14.8	15.2
Men living alone	5.6	8.6	9.7	10.2	10.7	11.2
Other family households	10.6	12.9	14.8	15.6	16.0	16.4
Married couples without children	30.3	29.9	29.8	28.9	28.7	28.2
Married couples with children	40.3	30.9	26.3	25.5	24.1	23.3

Source: U.S. Census Bureau, Current Population Survey, March Supplements: 1970–2003

A COUPLE'S RIGHT TO PRIVACY

In 2003, the Supreme Court held that a Texas sodomy statute prohibiting two men from engaging in sexual conduct violated the plaintiffs' due process rights (*Lawrence v. Texas*). A majority of the Court said:

The petitioners are entitled to respect for their private lives. The State cannot demean their existence or control their destiny by making their private sexual conduct a crime. Their right to liberty under the Due Process Clause gives them the full right to engage in their conduct without intervention of the government.

Justice O'Connor concurred in the result, stating that the Texas statute violated principles of equal protection because it outlawed homosexual sodomy, but not heterosexual sodomy. Justices Scalia, Rehnquist, and Thomas dissented, arguing that a prohibition of sodomy does not infringe on a fundamental right—that "[w]hat Texas has chosen to do is well within the range of traditional democratic action."

AGREEMENTS TO SHARE EXPENSES OR PROPERTY

An unmarried couple living together can agree to share expenses or acquire property. The fact that two people are living together does not make the agreement automatically enforceable. Gener-

 TO SUE OR NOT TO SUE

What should you do when a relationship is over and the other person hasn't stuck to the agreements you both made? If you stand to lose a large amount of money or property, then a lawsuit or the threat of a lawsuit may be worthwhile. If the amount involved is relatively small, however, the wiser course of action probably is to walk away—hopefully having gained some wisdom for dealing with your next relationship. Similarly, if there is no practical way to collect the amount you are owed—if, for example, the person in question has virtually no assets or steady source of income—a lawsuit is not likely to be worth the effort.

ally, if an agreement between two people who are not living together would be enforceable, then a similar agreement between two people who are living together will also be enforceable.

Thus, if two people wish to agree about how much each will pay for rent, mortgage, utilities, groceries, auto expenses, and so forth, they can enter into a valid and enforceable agreement. If one party does not keep his or her end of the bargain, the other party can sue. A lawsuit, however, is generally a sure sign that the relationship has fallen apart.

In some cases, an unmarried couple may be deemed to have a business relationship as well as a personal relationship. This type of combined relationship can create legal rights. In an Oregon case, for example, an unmarried couple agreed to operate a ranch together and share equally in the resulting profits and expenses. When the couple split up, a court ruled that each partner was entitled to one-half of the ranch's increase in value during the time they lived and worked together—regardless of the fact that one of the partners was not actually the owner of the ranch.

As is the case with any contract, agreements between unmarried couples should be specific and in writing. Though oral agreements might be enforceable, such agreements generally will be much harder to prove.

In order to be valid, contracts usually require **consideration**. This means that, in exchange for entering into the contract, each party should provide some benefit to the other—for example, by agreeing to pay a portion of the couple's living expenses. Keep in mind that if an agreement appears to constitute a gift from one party to the other—that is, if one party appears to receive all of the benefits stemming from the agreement, without offering anything in return—the agreement might be unenforceable due to lack of consideration.

THE "I'LL-TAKE-CARE-OF-YOU" PROMISE

Lawyers and judges refer to certain types of agreements as "pillow talk"—agreements made by couples during moments of intimacy, when one member of the couple may feel insecure about the future. The other person may offer reassurance in the form of such promises as: "Don't worry," "I love you," "I'll take care of you," or "Everything will be OK." All too often, however, everything does not turn out OK. Often, one member of the couple decides to end the relationship, and the more vulnerable party does not feel taken care of after all.

In this type of situation, does the more vulnerable partner have any recourse? If a person feels that his or her continued care is uncertain, and if that person files a lawsuit to collect on the other party's "pillow talk" promises, is she or he likely to succeed?

In a nutshell: No.

To begin with, such agreements rarely are in writing, so their existence can be difficult to prove in court. In fact, some states require that such agreements be in writing in order to be enforceable.

Moreover, a promise that "I'll take care of you" or "Everything will be OK" probably is too vague to be enforceable. Courts do not have clear standards for determining the meaning of such promises, and in the absence of a clear agreement between parties, courts are reluctant to create the terms of a contract. The vague promises quoted above are not nearly as specific as, say, an agreement to pay half the rent or to share equally the profits and expenses of running a ranch.

Third, even if a "pillow talk" promise is specific, it could still be viewed as contingent on circumstances that no longer exist. If such promises mean anything, they probably mean: "I'll support you financially as long as we remain a couple." If a couple breaks up after exchanging such a promise, a court probably would find that the implied conditions of the promise—in this example, that the parties remain a couple—have not been met, and that there thus exists no enforceable agreement for continued support.

Fourth, such agreements may be unenforceable for lack of consideration. As discussed earlier in this chapter, contracts usually require that each party provide some benefit to the other in order for a valid agreement to exist. In the case of many

AGREEMENTS TO LIVE TOGETHER: TWO EXAMPLES

Bob and Carol have dated for four months, and decide they want to live together without getting married. They plan to continue their jobs—Bob as a salesperson at a department store, and Carol as a junior high school teacher. They decide to formalize their relationship and responsibilities in writing. Carol and Bob prepare and sign a two-page statement in which they agree to share equally in living expenses: rent for a new apartment they'll obtain together, electricity, gas, groceries, and telephone, with each paying for his or her own long-distance calls. The agreement also states that each will be responsible for his or her personal expenses, such as clothes and car payments.

If Bob and Carol break up one year later and one of them has not paid his or her share of the expenses, their agreement probably will be legally enforceable.

Ted and Alice meet at a dance where Ted is a member of the band and Alice is a guest. After dating Ted for two days, Alice moves in with him. It seems like a match made in heaven: they travel often, and both love staying up late at night. Alice quits her part-time job as a secretary, though Ted continues to work with his successful band. Two months into their relationship, in a romantic moment at 3 A.M., Ted says to Alice: "This is great! I'll take care of you, and I hope we'll always be together!" But four months later, Ted meets a woman with whom he prefers to spend his time, and he asks Alice to move out.

If Alice sues for support and for half of what Ted earned during their relationship, she is likely to lose. Their agreement is not specific enough. In particular, Alice did not specifically agree to give something—say, a specified share of the rent payments—in order to obtain particular benefits from Ted. In addition, courts do not view companionship—and especially sex—as the basis for an enforceable agreement between two people who live together.

"pillow talk" agreements, however, the relevant promises might be viewed as unilateral or gratuitous: one partner promised to take care of the other, but there was no specific promise offered in return. The partner seeking support might argue that he or she promised to maintain the home or provide emotional support in exchange for a promise of financial security. However, such promises are not likely to be specific enough to be deemed enforceable, and may be viewed—as is discussed above—as contingent on continuation of the relationship. In general, courts are more inclined to enforce agreements for the exchange of tangible consideration—payment of expenses, for example, or rights to property.

Keep in mind that courts will not enforce agreements to provide financial support in exchange for sexual relations, as such agreements are viewed as uncomfortably close to contracts for prostitution.

HEALTH-CARE POWERS OF ATTORNEY

People living together may be concerned about who will have the power to make decisions about their health care in the event that they are unable to make such decisions themselves—if, for example, they become unconscious due to accident or illness.

If you want to authorize the person with whom you live to make health-care decisions on your behalf, you should prepare and sign a **health-care power of attorney**. By signing this form, you designate an individual to make decisions on your behalf, in the event that you are unable to do so, about the administration or discontinuation of health care. You may also use this form to specify limits on the decision-making power of the person you designate—if, for example, you do not want a particular type of treatment or do not want your organs donated in the event of your death. In the absence of a health-care power of attorney, health-care decisions probably would be left to relatives, such as your parents, siblings, or adult children.

A person who holds power of attorney usually is entitled to

TALKING TO A LAWYER

Q. *I live with my partner. If he were hospitalized, wouldn't I automatically have the right to make decisions about his health care?*

A. No. If your partner is unable to make health-care decisions for himself, doctors will consult any documents he has executed specifically to address that contingency—for example, a health-care power of attorney or living will. If no such document exists, doctors will consult only persons with a legal relationship to your partner—parents, siblings, and so on. The priority given to your relationship for these purposes may vary from state to state.

Answer by Judge Jerelyn D. Maher, Tremont, Illinois

Q. *The man who was my "steady" moved in with me when his lease was up. He promised to pay half the rent on my apartment. He paid half the first month's rent, but nothing else. He moved out two months later. Can I force him to pay his share of the last two months' rent?*

A. If the promise was oral only, then the agreement is probably not enforceable. In addition, there seems to have been no consideration offered in exchange for the promise of rent—except perhaps for simple companionship, which alone normally does not create an enforceable agreement.

Answer by Judge Jerelyn D. Maher, Tremont, Illinois

access the patient and his or her medical records. However, he or she is not obligated to pay the patient's medical bills.

If you designate a person to hold power of attorney for your health care, inform that person of your choice and discuss the circumstances under which life support should be continued or stopped. This will make it easier for your designee to make an appropriate decision should the need arise. Keep the original document in a safe place, and keep a copy with your other important documents. You should also give a copy of the form to your agent and your doctors and, if possible, bring a copy with you whenever you are admitted to the hospital.

WILLS

People who live together in a committed relationship may wish to draw up wills naming each other as beneficiaries, at least with respect to certain items. If, for example, the couple acquired property for its mutual use, such as furniture and appliances, each party may wish to leave his or her interest in the property to the other in the event of death. Members of a couple also may wish to leave other types of property to each other, such as cash or belongings with sentimental value. In the absence of a will that makes such a bequest, the property of the deceased most likely would pass to his or her blood relatives—and not to the surviving partner—upon death. Thus, to ensure that each member of a couple is provided for as the other intends, it is important that they both prepare wills.

If you have doubts about the duration of your relationship, but wish to leave something to your partner if you are still together when you die, you can make a bequest that is contingent on your living together at the time of your death. Then, if you and your partner are still living together when you die, the will would make the bequest as you intended. If you are not living together, the bequest would not be made, or perhaps an alternative bequest would be made in its place.

If you and your partner hold titled property such as a house, condominium, or car in joint tenancy with right of survivorship, a will would not be necessary to pass that property to your partner. Property held in such tenancy will pass automatically to the surviving joint tenant. Jointly held bank and investment accounts also pass to the surviving partner.

Another issue to consider when drafting a will is responsibility for making funeral arrangements. If two people who live together want to designate each other as the persons responsible for their funeral arrangements, they should say so in their wills. Otherwise, the responsibility and right of making funeral arrangements probably will fall to a blood relative. Payment of funeral expenses generally is made from the **estate**—that is, the money and property—of the person who dies, assuming that person left behind enough money or property to cover such expenses.

In addition to specifying responsibility for funeral arrangements in a regular will, you also may wish to specify such responsibility in a living will. A **living will** is a document in which you leave instructions to be followed in the event you are incapacitated and cannot express your desires. For example, a living will might indicate that you do not want artificial life support, such as a respirator or feeding tube, in the event of irreversible coma or the final stage of a terminal illness. A living will also could describe factors you would like considered in deciding whether or not to continue life support or initiate a new treatment. Such factors might include: the level of mental function to which you would return if there were a recovery; the degree to which you needed help with feeding and toileting; the amount of pain you were experiencing; or any opportunities for relatives or friends to visit you before your death. Since living wills are designed to be read before the time of death, they can be a useful forum for expressing your wishes about funeral arrangements, thus increasing the likelihood that those wishes will be followed. (Sometimes regular wills are not read until after a person's funeral.)

If you do not want to sign a living will, but want to increase the likelihood that funeral instructions in your regular will are followed, tell your partner, family, and close friends the location of your will, and inform them that your funeral instructions are included therein.

Yet another way of handling funeral arrangements is to enter into a prearrangement contract with a funeral home. Such a contract might provide for the manner of payment—and may even allow for advance payment—of funeral expenses, and might include a description of the type of funeral that should be held.

ENGAGEMENT RINGS

If an engagement is broken off, what happens to the engagement ring? Normally, it should be returned to the person who gave it. The ring usually is viewed as a gift given in anticipation of marriage. If the marriage will not take place, the condition on which the gift was given has not been met. Thus, the gift should be returned. This is particularly true if the person who received the ring broke off the engagement. In some states, if the giver of the ring broke off the engagement, the person who received the ring is entitled to keep it.

If the parties have given each other presents during the course of their relationship—such as birthday or holiday presents—those gifts normally do not have to be returned. Such presents usually are viewed as an unconditional gifts, such as those made between friends. Once an unconditional gift is given, the recipient is entitled to keep it, unless the person making the gift placed a clear condition on the gift when presenting it.

THE WORLD AT YOUR FINGERTIPS

- More information about laws affecting people who live together, and lists of issues that might be covered in a contract signed by two such people, can be obtained from Nolo at *www.nolo.com*. (Click on "Family Law.")
- You can also find information about laws affecting people who live together at the Findlaw website, at *http://public.findlaw.com/family.*
- The Alternatives to Marriage Project is a national organization that offers general support to people who choose not to marry, or who are unable to marry; for more information, access *www.unmarried.org*.
- Many gay rights organizations offer publications and other information about the legal rights and needs of people who are in committed, unmarried relationships. A good place to start is

the Lambda Legal Foundation website at *www.lambdalegal.org*. Click on "The Issues" to access a full list of topics.

REMEMBER THIS

• If two people are planning on living together, it usually is a good idea for them to have explicit discussions about how they will share expenses. If they wish to be particularly clear about the agreement and increase the likelihood that it will be an enforceable legal obligation, the agreement should be in writing and signed by both parties.

• People who live together do not have the same legal protections and obligations as married people, but they can sign certain documents and enter into agreements to provide extra protections for each other. For example, unmarried couples can hold property, such as a home or car, in joint tenancy with right of survivorship; leave money or property to each other in a will; and grant each other health-care powers of attorney to make decisions in the event that one of them becomes incapacitated.

CHAPTER 5

Financial Aspects
of Marriage

Barbara and Tom are getting married. Their finances, which generally have remained separate, now will be more closely linked—when, for example, they buy a house together, open a joint checking account, apply for credit cards, and file joint tax returns. What are their new rights and obligations?

If a couple divorces, the classification of property is an important factor in deciding how that property will be divided. This chapter presents general rules regarding classification of property and debts. Keep in mind, however, that all rules have exceptions and that laws may vary from state to state.

Most property that is acquired during a marriage is considered **marital** or **community property**. For example, wages earned by a husband and wife during their marriage generally are considered marital property. If one or both spouses buy a house or establish a business during the marriage, that house or business usually will be considered marital property, particularly if it is purchased with the earnings of both spouses.

Separate or **nonmarital property** is property that one spouse owned before the marriage. Separate property also includes inheritances and gifts—except, in many cases, gifts between spouses—acquired by one spouse during the marriage. During and after the marriage, each spouse may keep control of his or her separate property—meaning that he or she is free to buy, sell, or borrow money against that property. Income earned from separate property, such as interest, dividends, or rent, is generally considered separate property, though in some states it may be considered marital property.

Similarly, if property **appreciates**—that is, increases in value—during the marriage, the amount of the increase may be classified as separate property, though in some states it may be classified as marital property. Ultimately, this classification may depend on the type of effort, if any, expended by the couple to produce the increase in value. If the effort was **passive**—as in the case of appreciating stocks—the value of the increase is more likely to be classified as separate, or nonmarital, property. If, on the other hand, the increase was the result of **active** efforts—such as efforts expended in managing a business—the value of the increase would more likely be classified as marital property.

Separate property can become marital property if it is mixed with marital property. Suppose, for example, that a wife owns an apartment building she purchased before her marriage. If she deposits rent checks into a joint checking account she shares with her husband, that rent money can become marital property—though the building is likely to remain the wife's separate property as long as she keeps it in her name. If the wife adds her husband's name to the building's title, that could convert the building into marital property.

In addition, if one spouse devotes a great deal of effort to maintaining the other spouse's separate property, that effort could be sufficient to convert the separate property into marital property—or it could give the spouse who expended the effort a right to some form of payback. Likewise, if during a marriage

 TALKING TO A LAWYER

Q. If I inherit $50,000 from a family member and place the money in an investment account that my spouse and I set up five years ago, is the inheritance still mine or does it become marital property?

A. By voluntarily placing the money in a marital account, you have commingled your inheritance with a marital asset. As a result, you are making a gift to the marriage and the inheritance will be considered marital property.

Answer by Judge Jerelyn D. Maher, Tremont, Illinois

one spouse devotes significant effort to maintaining his or her separate property, that effort also could create an obligation to pay back the marital estate. Chapter 10 will discuss further how courts divide marital property in a divorce.

A husband and wife may own property together during their marriage. This occurs automatically in the nine **community property states**: Arizona, California, Idaho, Louisiana, Nevada, New Mexico, Texas, Washington, and Wisconsin, as well as Puerto Rico. These jurisdictions hold that each spouse owns equally the income earned and property acquired during a marriage. This is true even if one spouse supplies all the income.

DEBTS

A husband and wife may be responsible for debts incurred by one or the other of them individually, depending on the nature of such debts and where the couple resides. More specifically, if both a husband and wife have co-signed for a debt, both will be responsible for paying it. For instance, assume a husband and wife apply together for a charge card. If both sign the application form and promise to pay the charge bills, both will be responsible for paying off the balance to the credit card company or store, even if only one of them makes the purchases and the other disapproves. If a husband and wife have co-signed a mortgage to buy a home, both of them are potentially liable to the mortgage company, even if one of them no longer lives in the home. Similarly, in community property states, one spouse may be responsible for debts incurred by the other.

A husband and wife also can be held responsible for each other's debts, even if they have not co-signed for them, if the debts are considered **family expenses**. Some states have **family expense statutes** that render a husband or wife liable for expenses incurred for the benefit of the family, even if the other spouse did not sign for or approve such expenses in advance. Still other states impose the family expense obligation by common law without a statute. Thus, if a wife in one of these states

FORMS OF PROPERTY OWNERSHIP

Spouses who share property generally enjoy one of three forms of co-ownership:

Joint tenancy. A form of ownership that exists when two or more people own property that includes a **right of survivorship**. Each person has the right to possess the property. If one partner dies, the survivor becomes the sole owner. Any two people—not just spouses—may own property as joint tenants. A creditor may claim the debtor's interest in joint tenancy property—in other words, a creditor can force the sale of joint property to satisfy the debt of a single joint tenant.

Tenancy by the entirety. Allowed only in some states, tenancy by the entirety is a type of co-ownership of property by a husband and wife. Like joint tenancy, it includes a right of survivorship. But a creditor of one spouse may not **attach** (seize) the property to satisfy the debt of just one tenant. Thus, tenancy by the entirety provides more protection for the owners than joint tenancy. Each party usually must consent to the sale of the property. Divorce may result in a division of the property held in tenancy by the entirety, as well as division of property held in other types of tenancy.

Tenancy in common. This form of co-ownership gives each person control over his or her share of the property, and the shares need not be equal. The law does not limit tenancy in common to spouses. A tenancy in common has no right of survivorship; when one spouse dies, his or her share passes to the applicable heirs, either by will or in accordance with state laws.

Tenancy rules vary from one state to another. Some tenancies are complex and must be created in a precise manner; otherwise the courts may not enforce them.

charges groceries at a local store or takes her child to a doctor for care, her husband could be liable for the expenses because they were incurred for the benefit of the family.

On the other hand, if one spouse incurs debt solely for his or her personal benefit—if, say, a wife runs up bills for a personal holiday, or a husband buys expensive coins for his coin collection—the other spouse normally will not be liable unless he or she co-signed for the debt, benefited from the purchase, or approved the purchase. Such debts are likely to be viewed as benefiting only one party; therefore, that party's spouse will not be liable for the debt in states that are not community property states, as most states are not. In community property states, however, one spouse generally is liable for the debts of the other.

In both community property and non-community property states, one spouse generally is not liable for debts brought into the marriage by the other spouse. Instead, such debts belong to the spouse who incurred them.

In many states, however, there is an exception to this general rule: A debt incurred before marriage—including a child support debt—can be collected against the joint property of a new marriage. Thus, for example, if a man owes $15,000 in support to the children of his first marriage, and also owns a house or bank account in joint tenancy with his second wife, those assets might be seized by a court to pay off the old support debt.

If one spouse owns a business and the other does not, the spouse who does not own the business normally will not be li-

---

 SECOND SPOUSES BEWARE

If a second spouse is worried about a first spouse or other creditors from a first marriage placing a claim on the assets of a second marriage, that second spouse should keep most of his or her property in his or her own name rather than in joint tenancy with the new spouse.

able for business debts, unless the non-owner co-signed on the debt or the couple resides in a community property state.

It is common for institutions that lend money to small businesses to require personal guarantees of payment not only from the businesses themselves, but also from the owners of those businesses. (In the event a business debt is not paid, lenders prefer the option of reaching into as many pockets as possible.) If the owner of a business also owns a home, the lender may want the home to serve as collateral for a business loan. This means that both the business owner and his or her spouse may be asked to sign a paper allowing use of the home as collateral. If the business cannot pay off its debts, the couple may lose their home.

Wives and husbands are entitled to open credit accounts in their individual names. Creditors cannot require a spouse to cosign for an account unless the party seeking credit lives in a community property state—in which case both signatures can be required, since spouses in such states are liable for debts incurred by either of them during the marriage.

TAXES

If a husband's and wife's names and signatures appear on a state or federal personal income tax return, both are liable for the taxes. If a couple files jointly, the Internal Revenue Service generally holds each spouse responsible for the entire tax debt.

In some circumstances, a spouse who signs a joint tax return can be excused from liability if he or she can prove that he or she is an **innocent spouse**. A wife or husband may be considered an innocent spouse if he or she did not know—and had no reason to know—that a tax return understated the amount of tax actually due.

This lack of knowledge, however, is often hard to prove. For example, the *Wall Street Journal* reported a case in which the wife of an IRS auditor did not know that her husband was taking bribes—but neither did she ask how the couple could afford certain luxuries, such as expensive educations for their children

FOR MAXIMUM PROTECTION

If a married person wants full protection against possible liability for inaccurate tax returns filed by his or her spouse, the best approach is to file as "married filing separately." If the husband and wife have roughly equal incomes, their combined taxes will be about the same whether they file "married filing separately" or "married filing jointly." If, however, there is a significant difference in their incomes, their combined taxes are likely to be less if they file jointly rather than separately.

and country club dues, on her husband's modest government salary. The wife, as well as her husband, was found liable for $150,000 in unpaid taxes and penalties. (Her husband also went to jail.)

On the other hand, the IRS provides the following example of a case in which a taxpayer would be entitled to partial protection as an innocent spouse:

> At the time you signed your joint return, you knew that your spouse did not report $5,000 of gambling winnings. The IRS examined your tax return several months after you filed it and determined that your spouse's unreported gambling winnings were actually $25,000. You established that you did not know about, and had no reason to know about, the additional $20,000 because of the way your spouse handled gambling winnings. The understatement of tax due to the $20,000 will qualify for innocent spouse relief if you meet the other requirements. The understatement of tax due to the $5,000 of gambling winnings will not qualify for relief.

In years past, a "**marriage penalty**" existed—a higher level of federal taxes was levied on married people than on single people living in the same circumstances. In 2004, the marriage penalty was eliminated, for the most part, and couples now pay approximately the same total amount of taxes whether they are married or unmarried.

GIFTS BETWEEN SPOUSES

A person may make gifts of any amount to his or her spouse without paying federal gift taxes, as long as the recipient spouse is a U.S. resident. However, such gifts must be outright gifts—that is, not given in exchange for some benefit—or must be made through a trust. Most, but not all, state laws have done away with taxes on gifts between spouses.

The same is not true, however, of gifts made to other family members or persons outside the family. Gifts to children, other relatives, people outside the family, and trusts may be taxable if their value exceeds a certain amount per year. As of 2005, federal tax law allows a person to give someone other than a spouse up to $11,000 per year without the recipient having to pay any tax on the gift. A married couple could give $22,000 each year to, say, their child without that child having to pay a gift tax. However, if the total gifts exceed a certain dollar amount, the estate tax credit available to the donor could be reduced. Estate taxation is a changing area of the law; a tax consultant or a lawyer specializing in gifts and estates can provide up-to-date information.

DOING BUSINESS TOGETHER

Wives and husbands can, of course, do business together. They can be business partners, just like any other two people. They can set up a corporation, and both can be owners and employees of the corporation. They can also form a partnership, or one spouse can own a business and employ the other. And they can compensate one another with wages and benefits, including health insurance and retirement plans, just as they would any other employee.

If wages and benefits are paid to a spouse or child, the value of such wages and benefits generally should not exceed reasonable or fair market value. If artificially high payments are made, the business could get into trouble with the Internal Revenue Service.

THE WORLD AT YOUR FINGERTIPS

• For information about the legal implications for married couples of buying and selling homes, see the American Bar Association LawInfo site at: *www.abalawinfo.org/hom1.html*.

• For further information about marital and community property and other family law questions, see the FreeAdvice website at *http://family-law.freeadvice.com/divorce_law/*.

• You can obtain tax information from the Internal Revenue Service. Call 1-800-829-1040, or visit their website at *www.irs.gov.*

REMEMBER THIS

• Money earned and other property acquired during a marriage—including wages and pensions—are generally considered marital or community property. A court can divide that property between spouses at the time of a divorce.

• Money earned and other property acquired before a marriage, or received by inheritance during a marriage, are usually considered nonmarital or separate property. Such property usually can be kept by the person who acquired it, so long as the money or property is kept in the person's own name and is not mixed with marital or community property.

• Persons who are married may be responsible for the debts of their spouses incurred during the marriage, particularly if the debts are for family expenses.

CHAPTER 6

Having Children

A married couple has been trying to conceive a child for three years without success. The couple is considering additional ways of having a child, including in vitro fertilization and hiring a surrogate mother. What are the legal issues associated with these options?

The decision to have a child is protected by the **right of privacy** under the **Fourteenth Amendment** to the United States Constitution. Individuals who wish to have children cannot be barred from doing so—unless, perhaps, they are incarcerated. Individuals who do not wish to have a child have a legal right to obtain and use contraceptives, and to have an abortion.

If a woman becomes pregnant, neither her partner nor the courts can force her to have an abortion. The decision of whether to continue a pregnancy belongs solely to the woman.

Similarly, a person cannot legally force his or her spouse to have a child. If one spouse wants to have a child, but the other does not, that disagreement could constitute an "irreconcilable difference" under the no-fault divorce laws of most states, and thus could be grounds for a divorce. In states where divorce requires that one or both parties be at fault, disagreement on the question of whether to have children might be deemed "mental cruelty," and thus could constitute the basis for ending a marriage.

MEDICALLY ASSISTED PREGNANCIES

There are a variety of medically assisted means by which individuals can become parents, including artificial insemination and in vitro fertilization (IVF). These procedures have legal implications that vary by state. Generally, however, if both husband and wife consent to artificial insemination or in vitro fertilization, the rights and duties of the husband, wife, and child will be the same as if the child had been naturally conceived.

Surrogate Parenthood

In a **surrogate parenting arrangement**, a woman agrees—sometimes in exchange for payment, sometimes not—to bear a child for another couple. Parties usually enter into this type of arrangement when the wife cannot conceive or carry a child to term. In most surrogate parenting arrangements, artificial insemination enables the husband's sperm to fertilize an egg belonging to either the wife or surrogate mother. This makes the husband the biological father of the resulting child.

A surrogate mother agrees to give up all parental rights at birth. Then the wife of the biological father legally adopts the child. Most states outlaw arrangements in which the surrogate

 TALKING TO A LAWYER

Q. A married couple that is unable to have children would like to hire a woman to serve as a surrogate mother. In the proposed arrangement, the surrogate mother would be impregnated with the husband's sperm through artificial insemination, and the married couple would take custody of the child after birth. Is this arrangement legal? Would the surrogate mother be allowed to change her mind and keep the baby?

A. In most states, the surrogate mother could not be forced to give up the baby if she changed her mind. The biological father, however, would still have an equal right to custody of the child. Courts generally will not terminate the rights of either a father or surrogate mother without a showing of unfitness. Custody would be decided according to the best interests of the child.

Answer by Professor Barbara Atwood, Mary Ann Richey Professor of Law, University of Arizona, Tucson, Arizona

mother receives payment. Other states have laws that prohibit surrogate parenting arrangements entirely, or that grant surrogate mothers the right to keep their children after birth. Persons seeking to have a child by means of a surrogate parenting arrangement should seek legal advice before entering into such an agreement.

Custody of Frozen Embryos

For couples seeking to have a child through in vitro fertilization, an issue that may arise is: What should happen to frozen embryos—or **pre-embryos**—in the event that the couple splits up?

Generally, the first place couples should look to resolve issues relating to frozen embryos is the contract they signed with the fertility clinic. Such an agreement usually spells out what will happen to the embryos in the event of divorce or other circumstances, including the death of one or both parties or a change of mind by one or both parties. A couple generally has many options, and may agree to one or more of the following:

• implantation of frozen embryos, in the female partner only, with the recent consent of both parties;

• destruction of unused frozen embryos after a certain period of time;

• donation of unused embryos for medical research or treatment;

 EMBRYOS AND PRE-EMBRYOS

The definitions of "embryo" and "pre-embryo" vary, but the term "pre-embryo" often refers to a fertilized ovum in the first fourteen days after conception, before the cells begin to differentiate—at which point the pre-embryo becomes an embryo. A pre-embryo also has been defined as a fertilized ovum from the time of conception until it becomes implanted in the uterus, at which point it becomes an embryo.

- donation of unused embryos for implantation in another woman; or
- use of the embryos—or prohibition of such use—by one or both parties upon certain events, including death, separation, or divorce.

Only a moderate number of court cases and statutes have dealt with the issue of how to handle disputes over frozen embryos. One approach is to favor the desires of the partner who does not want to procreate over the desires of the partner who wants to procreate using the frozen embryos—unless the partner who wants to have a child has no reasonable alternative means of doing so. If, for example, a woman can no longer produce viable eggs, or if a man can no longer produce viable sperm, then the interests of that partner may outweigh the interests of the other. (See "A Tennessee Case Involving Frozen Embryos," below.)

 ## A TENNESSEE CASE INVOLVING FROZEN EMBRYOS

The 1992 case *Davis v. Davis* highlights just a few of the issues that may arise when a couple decides to freeze its embryos for later use.

Mary Sue Davis and Junior Lewis Davis met while they were both in the Army, stationed in Germany. They married and tried to have children. Mary Sue had five tubal pregnancies, at which point she decided to have her left fallopian tube ligated, thus leaving her without functional fallopian tubes by which she could conceive naturally. The couple then tried in vitro fertilization (IVF). In that procedure, ova were extracted from Mary Sue's ovaries, sperm was provided by Junior, the sperm and ova were mixed together in a petri dish, and the resulting pre-embryo was transferred to Mary Sue's uterus. Despite multiple attempts for more than three years, however, pregnancy did not result. After their final attempt at IVF, the Davises decided to store their remaining embryos using cryogenic preservation—in which the products of conception are preserved at subzero temperatures, generally with an eye to later attempts at fertilization.

Within three months of their last attempt at IVF, Junior filed for divorce. The couple agreed on all issues in the divorce except "custody" of their seven frozen embryos. Mary Sue initially sought custody of the embryos, stating that she intended to have them implanted in her own uterus in an attempt to become pregnant after the divorce. Junior said he would like the embryos kept in their frozen state until he decided if he wanted to become a parent without being married to Mary Sue.

While the case was still pending, Mary Sue and Junior both remarried—each to other persons—and their positions changed. Mary Sue no longer wanted the frozen embryos for her own use, but wanted the authority to donate them to a childless couple. Junior strongly opposed such a donation, and said he would prefer to have the frozen embryos discarded.

The Tennessee Supreme Court ruled that the right to privacy under the Constitution includes the right to procreate and the right to avoid procreation. When a couple differs about what should be done with frozen embryos, the court ruled that the prior agreement of the parties generally should be honored. In this case, Mary Sue and Junior had not agreed in advance about what to do with their frozen embryos. Thus, the court said it was necessary to balance their interests. "Ordinarily," said the court, "the party wishing to avoid procreation should prevail, assuming that the other party has a reasonable possibility of achieving parenthood by means other than the use of the preembryos in question." The court said that imposing unwanted parenthood on Junior would result in "financial and psychological consequences" that outweighed Mary Sue's desire to donate the pre-embryos to another couple. Thus, Mary Sue was unable to donate the pre-embryos over her former husband's objection.

ABORTION

In 1973, the Supreme Court held in *Roe v. Wade* that a woman has a constitutional right to seek an abortion before a fetus is viable outside her womb. The Court also ruled that states cannot require a woman to notify her husband before seeking an abortion. The Court was particularly concerned about the impact of a notification requirement on women in abusive relationships.

The Court reaffirmed *Roe v. Wade* in the 1992 case *Planned Parenthood v. Casey.* But although it reaffirmed a woman's right to seek an abortion early in pregnancy, the *Casey* Court also held that states may regulate many other aspects of abortion. After a fetus is viable, for example, states may prohibit abortions unless the mother's life or health is endangered. States also may impose a waiting period during which women may not obtain abortions unless their health is endangered. Specifically, the *Casey* Court upheld Pennsylvania's twenty-four-hour waiting period as a reasonable means of assuring that a woman seeking an abortion is making a deliberate decision. During that waiting period, the Court held that states also can require the providers of abortions to inform women about the risks of and alternatives to abortion.

The *Casey* Court also upheld a statute requiring parental consent for minors seeking an abortion. The statute in question allowed minors to forego seeking parental consent, and instead seek judicial permission, if the facts of the case supported a bypass of parental consent.

Keep in mind that the issues surrounding abortion—from the scope of regulation to the extent of government funding—may vary from state to state.

CHILDBIRTH

Parents generally are free to select the place at which their child will be born. They may choose a hospital, their own home, or a birthing center staffed by midwives, if such centers are available in their area. Some states allow nurse-midwives to deliver children at the parents' home or at a birthing center. Other states allow nurse-midwives to practice only at hospitals or under the direct supervision of a physician.

Under federal law, a hospital equipped to deliver babies is prohibited from turning away mothers in active labor, even if they are uninsured. This law, the **Emergency Medical Treatment and Active Labor Act**—also referred to as the **anti-**

dumping law—also prohibits hospitals from turning away other patients in urgent need of care.

As health-care technology improves and as health insurance companies seek to reduce the costs of health care, it is common for mothers and new babies to remain hospitalized for only short periods of time after delivery. The **Newborns' and Mothers' Health Protection Act** is a federal law that regulates insurance coverage of post-childbirth hospital stays. Under that law, group health plans, including health maintenance organizations (HMOs), must cover a hospital stay of at least forty-eight hours following a vaginal delivery and ninety-six hours following a delivery by cesarean section—though a woman's doctor, after consulting with the patient, may agree to an earlier discharge.

If a patient—or the parent of a patient—believes that a hospital stay should be longer than the insurance company or HMO is willing to cover, the patient or parent may appeal the decision to deny coverage. The patient's contract with the insurance company or HMO will specify the details of the appeals system. The first appeal generally is informal—a phone call or letter to the insurance company or HMO. If that appeal proves unsatisfactory, however, the patient usually may make a more formal appeal—for example, a hearing before administrators or physicians who work for the insurance company or HMO. If that appeal also fails, the patient might be entitled—depending on the nature of her contract and the state in which she lives—to seek outside relief, as through the court system or a neutral arbitrator.

The father or other family members may wish to be present for the delivery of a child. The decision of whether or not such persons are allowed in the delivery room normally is left to the hospital. Most hospitals permit fathers to be present during delivery. Many hospitals prefer that the father and mother go through some training before the delivery, such as a Lamaze class. Parents should check with their hospitals for other rules, and for information about which persons are allowed in the delivery room.

PATERNITY

A man who fathers a child by a woman to whom he is not married generally can acknowledge his **paternity** by signing the child's birth certificate—or another document—soon after the child's birth, in accordance with state laws.

If a man does not admit that a child is his, a woman can file suit against him to prove paternity and to obtain child support. In many states, fathers of children born out of wedlock also may be obliged to help pay medical expenses associated with pregnancy and delivery.

In some cases, a man wishes to claim paternity of a child born to a woman who is married to another man. In some states, the "outsider" may file a legal action to compel testing in order to establish biological paternity and parental rights. Paternity cases usually involve the use of scientific evidence. For example, DNA testing—typically conducted on swabs of tissue obtained from the mouth or from a blood sample—can prove to a near certainty whether a man is the father of a child.

RIGHTS AND RESPONSIBILITIES OF PARENTS

Parents have a right to control the care and upbringing of their children. This right gives parents the power to make various decisions affecting their children, including where they live, what schools they attend, what religion they follow, and what medical treatments they obtain.

Normally, states may not interfere in these decisions. Thus, only in life-threatening or extreme situations will the courts step in to overrule parents. For example, if parents refuse to provide lifesaving medical care to a dying child, a judge may make that child a ward of the court—or the state—and order that the care be provided. In some cases, parents have been prosecuted for withholding medical treatment from seriously ill children, even when the refusal was a result of their religious beliefs.

Both parents are obligated to support their child until the child reaches age 18 or graduates high school (through college in some states). Support for a child born out of wedlock is established using the same support guidelines as for a child whose parents are obtaining a divorce. In addition, a parent's duty to support a disabled child might continue for the child's entire life. Usually, the non-custodial parent pays support to the custodial parent. If an obligated parent refuses to support the child, a court can garnish wages, seize property and bank accounts, and even send the parent to jail. For further discussion of child support, see Chapter 12.

Parents also have the legal authority to control their children's behavior and social lives. As a result, parents may discipline or punish their children as they see fit—though they may not use cruel methods or excessive force. Such treatment would be considered child abuse, and could subject the parents to prosecution.

If a child injures another person or causes damage to another person's property, that child's parents may be liable for damages. Some states have statutes imposing liability on parents for vandalism caused by their children up to a certain dollar amount, such as $500 or $1,000. If a child's behavior is severely out of control, the state also may take custody of that child.

If a child has an accident while driving a parent's car, the parent's auto insurance policy generally will cover any loss to the same extent as if the parent had been driving—though parents usually must pay higher insurance premiums to cover young drivers.

Parents are legally responsible for their children until those children reach the age of majority (usually eighteen), marry, or leave home to support themselves.

NEGLECT AND ABUSE LAWS

Under state laws, it is a criminal offense if parents and legal guardians fail to meet children's basic needs—including food, clothing, shelter, medical treatment, and supervision. Such failure constitutes **child neglect**.

In addition, **child abuse** laws make it a crime for adults—including parents, legal guardians, other adults in the home, and baby-sitters—to abuse children in their care. Supervising adults may not administer physical punishment beyond what is considered reasonable. Thus, adults who beat children so severely that the children require medical treatment are in violation of these laws. Child abuse laws prohibit not only physical abuse and sexual abuse, but also emotional abuse, such as subjecting a child to extreme public humiliation.

Even if a person does not personally commit child abuse, that person may nonetheless be deemed guilty of abuse if he or she had legal responsibility for a child and failed to protect the child from an abuser. For example, a mother can be found guilty of child neglect or abuse if she allows a boyfriend to abuse her child.

The law compels a wide range of people who have contact with children to report suspected child abuse or neglect. Such people include doctors, nurses, teachers, child-care workers, and social workers. A person who is required to report suspected neglect or abuse could face civil or criminal penalties for failure to do so.

States often encourage the reporting of suspected abuse through special hot lines. To encourage persons to report abuse, most states offer immunity from **defamation** suits over reports made in **good faith**—meaning that if a person genuinely sus-

---

 DEFAMATION

Defamation is a written or oral statement that is false and causes harm to the reputation of another person. A court can award monetary damages if defamation is proved.

pects abuse, he or she cannot be sued by the accused abuser for reporting it, even if it later turns out that abuse did not occur.

Some states keep central lists of suspected child abuse cases. Such lists help to identify abusers, such as parents who take their children to different hospitals in order to conceal evidence of repeated abuse.

If the state removes a child from the home of an abusive or neglectful parent, it usually seeks to reunite the family after correction of the problems that led to removal. However, this is not always possible. If, for example, a parent makes little effort to improve or does not satisfactorily complete parenting-skills programs offered by the state, then the state may ask a court to terminate all parental rights. Federal law requires states to take steps toward such termination for parents whose children have been removed from the home for more than twelve months. If parental rights are terminated, the legal bonds between parents and child are completely and permanently severed. The child then may be adopted by another family.

RIGHTS OF CHILDREN

The law defines children as unmarried persons under the age of majority—usually eighteen—who have not left home to support themselves.

Children have a right to be supported by their parents. As mentioned earlier in this chapter, the right of support includes food, shelter, clothing, and medical care. Parents also are obliged to arrange for the education of their children, either at school or at home. If parents seek to educate their children at home, the parents usually must prove to the state that they offer a legitimate education program. Children taught at home may be subject to state testing to ensure that they are making satisfactory progress.

Children also have a right to public school education until graduation from high school—assuming they are not expelled from school for misconduct. In addition, under federal law, children with significant physical or mental disabilities have a right to government-paid special-education programs to meet their needs. If a parent believes that a child needs a special-education program, but the government is not providing one, the parent can appeal the issue through administrative agencies within the school system and through the courts if necessary.

Mature minors—generally defined as children over the age of twelve—are allowed to make their own decisions regarding certain medical procedures, even if parents disagree with those decisions. For example, in most states parents do not have absolute veto power over a minor's decision to use contraceptives or obtain an abortion. In many states, minors also can seek treatment for venereal disease without notification or consent of their parents. In addition, in some states, a mature minor can seek and obtain short-term mental-health treatment or counseling without parental consent.

If a child receives a large sum of money—such as through inheritance, payment of a damage award for a personal injury, or starring in a television series—the law protects that money by regulating how it is managed. Specifically, the law usually requires the appointment of a **guardian** to manage the child's finances. The guardian may be a parent or other person. In some cases there may be two guardians—one a parent and the other a non-family member, such as an attorney or bank officer. Guardians must ensure that a child's money is well managed and spent for the child's best interest; the money cannot be used for the primary benefit of other family members. If a guardian spends the money for his or her own benefit, or in some other way mismanages the funds, he or she will have violated a **fiduciary duty** to the child, and may be personally liable for the amount lost.

To help ensure that a child's money is properly invested and spent, a court may require a guardian to file periodic **accountings** with the court, itemizing the child's assets, explaining how the money has been spent, and outlining plans for future expenditures.

The law also allows children to sue—including, for example, for personal injuries suffered in an auto accident or a poorly maintained park. In most instances, the child's parent or legal guardian must begin the suit in the child's name.

Children accused of crimes are handled by their states' juvenile courts, and not by the regular criminal justice system. (In many states, however, children accused of serious crimes who are above a certain age—sometimes as low as thirteen—may be tried in court as adults.) Juvenile courts entitle children to only some of the procedural safeguards that adults receive, but juvenile courts have more freedom to deal with juveniles in an effort to rehabilitate them. A child on trial as a juvenile, for example, usually does not have the right to a jury trial, but the child generally may not be confined beyond the age of eighteen.

Children who are the subject of abuse and neglect proceedings are entitled to legal protections. Such protections usually include appointment of a **guardian ad litem** or an attorney for the child to present information to the court about what is best for that child. The guardian or attorney, for example, may present evidence to help the judge decide if a child should be returned to his or her parents, placed in a foster home, placed with a relative, or placed for adoption (if parental rights have been terminated).

DUTIES OF ADULT CHILDREN TOWARD THEIR PARENTS

Adult children normally have no legal responsibilities toward their parents. Their parents have no legal duties toward them. However, there are exceptions. In some states, children must support parents who are financially destitute. Children may be excused from payment if they cannot afford to support their parents, or if the parents have previously abandoned the child. In Montana, a child does not have to support an indigent parent if a judge or jury finds "the child is excused by reason of intemperance, indolence, immorality, or profligacy of the parent."

THE WORLD AT YOUR FINGERTIPS

- For more information about children's rights, visit the website of the ABA Center on Children and the Law at *www.abanet. org/child/home2.html.*
- For more information about women's health issues and abortion rights, visit the website of the Kaiser Family Foundation at *www.kff.org.* (Click on "Women's Health Policy.")
- For pro-choice perspectives, visit the NARAL Pro-Choice America website at *www.naral.org.* For pro-life perspectives, visit the National Right to Life website at *www.nrlc.org.*

REMEMBER THIS

- The right to have a child and the right to terminate a pregnancy are privacy interests protected by the Fourteenth Amendment to the U.S. Constitution.
- Custody rights and other legal issues associated with in vitro fertilization and surrogate parenting are governed by the agreements the parties sign, as well as by state law.
- A federal law—the Emergency Medical Treatment and Active Labor Act—requires hospitals to provide care for women in active labor. The Newborns' and Mothers' Health Protection Act provides that group health plans, including HMOs, must pay for hospital stays of at least forty-eight hours following vaginal deliveries and at least ninety-six hours following deliveries by cesarean section.

CHAPTER 7

Adoption

An unmarried eighteen-year-old becomes pregnant and wants to place her child for adoption. After the adoption, she also would like to know how the child is doing and perhaps have contact with him or her. What are her options?

E ach year in the United States, approximately 127,000 adoptions take place. The federal government divides adoptions into three categories: (1) **private agency, kinship,** and **tribal adoptions,** which include adoptions by stepparents; (2) **public agency adoptions;** and (3) **intercountry adoptions.** The first category is the largest, comprising 46 percent of all adoptions, though the percentage of such adoptions relative to other types has decreased over the last ten years. Public agency adoptions account for 39 percent of adoptions, and intercountry adoptions make up the remaining 15 percent, with approximately 19,000 adoptions each year by persons living in the United States. (See chart below.)

 ADOPTIONS IN THE U.S. BY TYPE IN 1992 AND 2001

	Private, kinship, or tribal	Public agency	Intercountry
1992 (total adoptions: 126,951)	77%	18%	5%
2001 (total adoptions: 127,407)	46%	39%	15%

Source: U.S. Department of Health and Human Services, National Adoption Information Clearinghouse, 2004 report.

RELATED ADOPTIONS

Related adoptions—in which one adoptive parent is related to the child by blood or marriage—are comparatively simple, assuming that no one objects. One of the most common types of adoptions is by a stepfather or stepmother. If the biological parent whom the stepparent "replaces" is living and consents to the stepparent adoption, there should be no problem. If he or she does not consent, however, the child may not be adopted unless a court finds that the biological parent is unfit or that other exceptional circumstances exist.

The definition of "unfit" varies from state to state, but the term normally refers not only to parents who have been abusive, neglectful, or convicted of serious crimes, but also to parents who fail to have regular contact with or support their children.

If an adoptive stepparent and a biological parent later obtain a divorce, that divorce will not affect the adoption. The adoptive stepparent continues to have all the rights and responsibilities of a biological parent, including a right to seek custody or visitation and a duty to support the child.

Similarly, an adopted child has all the rights of a biological child, including the right to inherit. If the child's adoptive parent leaves a will providing for his or her "children" without identifying those children by name, the adopted child will be treated the same as a biological child. If an adoptive parent dies without leaving a will, the adoptive child will receive the same share of any inheritance under state law as a biological child. In addition, in the event of an adoptive parent's death or disability, an adopted child is entitled to the same family insurance benefits and Social Security benefits as a biological child.

Adoption usually entails filing a written petition requesting the adoption, notifying persons who would be affected by the adoption—including the biological parents if they are alive—and appearing in court for a hearing. If the child to be adopted is above a certain age—generally twelve—his or her consent also may be necessary.

UNRELATED ADOPTIONS

Unrelated adoptions, in which the person adopting the child is not related to the child or the child's other parent, usually require more paperwork and more time to complete. Unrelated adoptions generally fall into two categories: **agency adoptions** and **private adoptions**.

Agency Adoptions

In agency adoptions, as the name implies, both biological and adoptive parents work through a licensed agency. The agency often supervises the care of biological mothers who are willing to place their children for adoption, and then assists in the placement of those children after birth. Agencies screen adoptive parents—often extensively—before an adoption proceeds. Some agencies have long waiting lists of parents. Some agencies also specialize in placing children born in foreign countries.

Agencies are licensed and regulated by the state, and often offer counseling or support services to adoptive families and biological parents after adoptions are completed.

Private Adoptions

Private adoptions bypass the use of agencies, and thus may help bypass the long waiting lists that can be typical of such agencies. Private adoptions are available in most states, but not all.

The process of private adoption begins when people who seek to adopt a child contact an attorney who specializes in adoptions. The attorney may work with physicians who know of women willing to place their children for adoption. Sometimes would-be parents will place ads in newspapers or on the Internet seeking women who are willing to place their babies for adoption. The ads might be placed by the adoptive parents directly or by their attorney.

In most states, adoptive parents are allowed to pay a biological mother's medical expenses and certain other costs during her pregnancy. But adoptive parents are not allowed to pay the biological mother specifically to place her child for adoption. Under the law, such payments constitute "black market adoption"—the literal buying and selling of children—and are a crime in every state.

Court procedures vary from state to state, but in all states court approval is necessary for both agency and private adoptions. Many states also require that adoptive parents be approved by a social-service agency.

Private adoptions are more complicated than unrelated adoptions. Thus, it is very important that proper consent be obtained from the biological parents—an issue that is discussed in the next two sections of this chapter. Assistance from an attorney licensed in the state where the adoption will take place is advisable.

CONSENTS

The Biological Mother

For an adoption to take place, the biological mother must consent to the adoption or her parental rights must have been terminated for other reasons, such as abuse or neglect of the child. The biological mother may be asked to sign a form before her child is born indicating that she plans to place the child for adoption. The form, however, is not binding.

The mother has the right to revoke her consent to an adoption for a certain period of time after the child is born. In most states, that window of time is relatively short—generally from forty-eight to seventy-two hours—although in some states it may be longer.

If a biological mother consents to adoption within a certain amount of time *after* the child's birth, it is much harder for her to revoke her consent. A biological mother generally may revoke an after-birth consent only if she can show that the consent was

MAKE SURE THE FATHER CONSENTS

Failure to obtain consent from a child's biological father has been at the center of some highly publicized adoption cases. For example, in the 1994 case *In re Petition of Doe,* a woman conceived a child, Baby Richard, out of wedlock. At the time of Baby Richard's birth, the biological mother and father were not living together. The mother lied to the father and told him that their child had died.

Meanwhile, the mother consented to termination of her parental rights and to adoption of the child. Later, the biological father learned the child was alive, and he sought to undo the adoption and gain custody of Baby Richard. The father filed his claim for custody fifty-seven days after Baby Richard's birth.

The case dragged through the Illinois courts for years while the child lived with his adoptive parents. When "Baby" Richard was three years old, the Illinois Supreme Court ruled that Richard had to be returned to his biological father, since the father had never consented to the adoption and had contested the adoption within two months of Richard's birth. The Illinois Supreme Court refused to consider the quality of the child's relationship with the adoptive parents or what was best for Richard. Instead, the court held the biological father was entitled to custody.

The court's decision caused an uproar in Illinois. The governor and many legislators objected to the decision. Although sympathetic to the biological father who had been deceived about the birth of his son, many people felt that the rights of the child and adoptive parents should have been treated as paramount. The legislature passed a statute requiring courts to consider the best interest of a child when deciding whether to rescind an adoption. But the Illinois Supreme Court refused to apply the statute retroactively to Richard's case, and stood by its order that Richard be returned to his biological father.

The case of Baby Richard illustrates the importance of obtaining consent from the biological father in order to help ensure that an adoption will not be undone. If a father who is not notified of his child's birth contests the adoption within the time period designated by state law, the adoptive parents might lose custody of that child. Many states are considering laws that would give greater protection to adoptive parents and the adoptive children who have bonded with them; but in the meantime, some states place more emphasis on the rights of biological fathers than on those of children or adoptive parents.

given as a result of **fraud** or **duress**. Fraud may have occurred if the adoption agency or attorney lied to the biological mother about the consequences of her consent. Duress may exist if a person at the adoption agency applied extreme emotional pressure to induce the mother to consent.

By itself, a biological mother's change of heart normally is not grounds for revoking an after-birth adoption consent. Although a mother may be under stress and feel emotionally drained after the birth of a child she plans to give up for adoption, courts generally do not view these reactions to the adoption as sufficient justification for revoking consent.

The Biological Father

For an adoption to take place, a biological father's consent is also necessary—at least if his identity is known. Thus, the biological father of a child to be placed for adoption should be notified of the birth and pending adoption so he may consent or object. If the father's identity is not known, the adoption may proceed without his consent—though adoptive parents generally can feel more confident about the validity of an adoption if the biological father has been notified and has consented.

If a biological father is not notified, he may later contest the adoption if he acts within a certain period of time—typically six months, though the amount of time varies between states—after the child's birth or adoption.

OTHER KINDS OF ADOPTION

Foreign Adoptions

Many prospective adoptive parents look to other countries in order to adopt a child. For couples or individuals seeking a child through this route, it is best to work with an agency or attorney experienced in foreign adoptions—with particular experience in the country from which the child is being sought. The adoptive parents will have to deal not only with U.S. regulations, but also with the regulations of the country from which the child is adopted.

Depending on how an adoption is set up, a child might be adopted by an American couple in his or her birth country before being brought to the United States, or the child might be brought to the United States with adoption proceedings taking place in an American court. Either way, entry of the child into the United States will need to be cleared with U.S. Citizenship and Immigration Services (USCIS).

USCIS requires that adoptive parents undergo a home study—an in-depth review of the prospective family and its home—by a licensed social worker, and that adoptive children receive medical exams before being brought into the United States.

Under the Child Citizenship Act of 2000, children adopted abroad automatically become U.S. citizens, provided that certain conditions are met. Such conditions include:

• that the child must have at least one parent who is a U.S. citizen, either by birth or naturalization;

• that the child be under eighteen years of age;

• that the child currently reside permanently in the United States, in the legal and physical custody of the parent who is a U.S. citizen; and

• that the child be a lawful permanent resident of the United States.

⚠ PROOF THAT A CHILD IS AN ORPHAN

As a condition of automatic U.S. citizenship for an adoptive child from a foreign country, U.S. Citizenship and Immigration Services also requires proof that the child is an **orphan**—which means that the child's biological parents must be dead or have voluntarily given up the child. If documentation to that effect cannot be obtained, the adoptive parents may find themselves stranded in the child's home country until documentation is obtained or a waiver is issued. In some countries, the persons or agencies providing children for adoption may submit forged documents in connection with an adoption. If USCIS suspects forgery, it may delay the process even further.

Interracial Adoptions

Interracial adoptions—particularly adoptions of African-American children by white parents—raise some of the most controversial issues in all of adoption law. In 1972, as just one example of the controversy such adoptions have generated, a spokesperson for the Association of Black Social Workers condemned interracial adoptions as "racial genocide."

Proponents of interracial adoptions note that there are tens of thousands of black children in foster care awaiting adoption, but not enough black families available to adopt them. Such proponents generally argue that a child is better off being adopted by a family of a different race than not being adopted at all.

Federal laws pertaining to **interethnic adoptions** provide that states shall diligently recruit "potential foster and adoptive families that reflect the ethnic and racial diversity of children in the State for whom foster and adoptive homes are needed." At the same time, federal law provides that persons and government agencies involved in adoption or foster care may not deny or delay placement of a child for adoption or foster care because of the prospective adoptive or foster parents' race.

Single-Parent Adoptions

Single persons may adopt children, although some agencies strongly prefer to place children with married couples. Other agencies—particularly those dealing with children who might be difficult to place—are willing to place children with single persons. Single-parent adoptions usually are possible as a form of private adoption.

As with an adoption sought by a couple, a single person who seeks to adopt a child must be approved by a social-service investigator and show that appropriate arrangements have been made for the child's care.

Adoption by Lesbian and Gay Couples

Most states allow gay and lesbian couples to adopt children, though in some states the law regarding such adoptions is unclear. If both members of a gay or lesbian couple adopt a child at the same time, the adoption is referred to as a **joint adoption**. If one partner adopts a child who is already the biological or adoptive child of the other partner, and if both partners will be acting as parents, the adoption is referred to as a **second-parent adoption**. As of 2005, states that allow second-parent adoptions by statute or by appellate-court decision include: California, Connecticut, Illinois, Indiana, Massachusetts, New York, New Jersey, Pennsylvania, and Vermont, as well as the District of Columbia.

Open Adoption

An **open adoption** is one in which the adoptive parents allow the biological mother or father continued contact with the child after the adoption. Such contact might take the form of periodic visits or the exchange of pictures and other information between the adoptive family and the biological parent or parents. The nature of the contact often is specified in the adoption agreement. Open adoptions have become more common, as more birth mothers have become involved in choosing the families that will adopt their children—particularly in the case of private adoptions.

Open adoptions are a relatively new phenomenon. In many states it is not certain whether open-adoption agreements are enforceable in the courts by birth mothers or fathers in the event that adoptive parents seek to discontinue contact with biological parents.

The uncertainty arises from the nature of traditional adoption laws. Adoption laws generally require that the parental rights of biological parents be terminated. Termination of parental rights traditionally has meant that biological parents have no more rights or responsibilities regarding their children. If a birth parent seeks to maintain contact with his or her child, that attempt might be viewed as an impermissible assertion of rights that no longer exist.

On the other hand, if adoptive parents agree to contact a child's biological parent or parents, and an adoption is understood to be contingent on such contact, the agreement might be enforceable. However, a biological parent should not count on such agreements being enforceable unless state law clearly indicates that this will be the case.

ADOPTION RECORDS

In most states, a court's adoption records are sealed and can be opened only by court order. Procedures and standards for opening records vary by state. Increasingly, states require that certain nonidentifying information, such as the medical history of biological families, be made available to adoptive parents at the time of adoption.

Some states have registries through which parties to an adoption can seek to contact each other. If, for example, a biological mother seeks to learn about her child, she may place her name, address, and telephone number in the registry. If an adopted child or adoptive parent seeks contact with the child's biological parents, they may also place their names in the registry. If the registry finds a "match"—that is, if the registry determines that parties to the same adoption are seeking information about one another—it will provide the parties with information to facilitate contact.

Oregon has a law that allows adopted children to obtain their adoption records, even if their biological parents expected their identities would not be revealed at the time the adoptions took place.

LEGAL ACTION FOR WRONGFUL ADOPTION

Under the law of many states, if an adoption agency has adverse information about a child who is being considered for adoption, the agency has an obligation to provide that information to a prospective adoptive family—particularly if the family requests such information. If the agency does not provide the information, it could be liable for any resulting damages. A lawsuit for such damages sometimes is referred to as an action for **wrongful adoption**.

In one such case, an agency withheld information about a biological mother's mental illness and institutionalization. As her child grew, the adoptive parents realized that the child had a severe mental illness requiring substantial treatment. The adoptive parents were able to collect damages for the cost of treatment and for their own emotional suffering.

In states that allow adoptive parents to seek damages from agencies for wrongful adoption, the law does not require that an agency guarantee the health of a child. However, the law does require that, if an agency has significant adverse information about a child—such as information about the child's health and genetic background—it must share that information with the adoptive parents.

TALKING TO A LAWYER

Q. Is it more difficult to adopt a child from another country than from the United States? Are there differences in costs?

A. There are several differences between international adoptions and domestic adoptions. In a domestic adoption, birth parents choose the adoptive parents for their child. In international adoptions, birth parents very rarely play a role in their child's adoption, and usually have relinquished parental rights to the child by the time he or she arrives at an orphanage. By the time the adoption is finalized on foreign soil, the relinquishment is irreversible. This means that the adoption is final—period, end of statement.

The sheer number of children available for international adoption makes a positive outcome virtually certain for qualified parents: You will be parents of a child if you can satisfy the foreign government's requirements. Usually, you can count on this happening within twelve to eighteen months. However, you should not consider international adoption if you are not ready to parent a child with special needs or developmental delays. Most, but not all, children adopted internationally have at least mild developmental delays.

Depending upon the foreign program you choose, the cost difference between a domestic adoption and an international adoption can be significant. The fees for services in domestic adoptions can range from less than $10,000 to as high as $40,000, depending upon birth parent expenses, medical costs, and the like. In an international adoption, the fees range from $20,000 to $35,000. Some of the reasons for the high cost of international adoption include: private, in-country legal fees that can add up to thousands of dollars; difficulty of finding qualified, highly reputable people to prepare a child's legal documents in a foreign country; and often astronomical travel costs resulting from the need to travel at the last minute and the inability to use frequent-flyer miles or discount fares. Your total costs may include a so-called orphanage donation, which helps feed and clothe the children who remain in the orphanage.

Answer by Harlan Tenenbaum,
Chair, Adoption Committee,
ABA Family Law Section, Wilmington, Delaware

A. The difficulty and cost of adopting a child from another country depend largely on the laws of the country from which the child is adopted. Many countries, for example, require that the adopting parents travel to the country at least once to adopt the child, and may require an in-country stay of several weeks. An agency or attorney with experience in international adoptions should be able to advise you on the requirements and costs associated with adoptions from different countries. The U.S. State Department also offers country-specific information for international adoptions.

Answer by James Landman,
Associate Director, American Bar Association
Division for Public Education, Chicago, Illinois

THE WORLD AT YOUR FINGERTIPS

• More information about different types of adoptions and lists of licensed adoption agencies can be obtained from The National Adoption Information Clearinghouse, operated by the U.S. Department of Health and Human Services, at *http://naic. acf.hhs.gov.*

• Federal statutes and regulations relating to adoption are available from the Legal Information Institute of Cornell University at *www.law.cornell.edu/topics/adoption.html.*

• The ABA Family Law Section has an Adoption Committee that offers information about adoption at *www.abanet.org/family/ committees/adoption.html.*

REMEMBER THIS

• If the biological parents of a child are alive, then they must consent to an adoption before it can take place. Alternatively, the parental rights of the biological parents must be terminated, or good faith efforts to locate the parents must have failed.

• Adoption of children from other countries requires compliance with the laws of the other countries as well as with the rules of the U.S. Citizenship and Immigration Services.

• Laws regarding open adoptions, in which biological parents maintain contact with their child after adoption, as well as adoptions by same-sex couples, vary from state to state.

CHAPTER 8

Deciding Whether
or Not to Divorce

The lead feature in each issue of Ladies' Home Journal *is a column entitled "Can This Marriage Be Saved?", which the Journal bills as "[t]he most popular, enduring women's magazine feature in the world."*

The feature has three sections. The first section is "The Wife's Turn," in which a wife recounts the frustrations of her marriage and why she is considering divorce. The husband then takes a turn discussing his unhappiness. (The husband usually comes across as being more at fault than the wife.) Finally, a counselor analyzes the couple's relationship, discussing why they have reached an impasse and what can be done to save their marriage. In Ladies Home Journal, *the marriage always is saved.*

In real life, of course, marriage counselors do not save all marriages. But they can help save *some* marriages, and they also can help wives and husbands with individual growth, regardless of whether they decide to divorce.

DECIDING WHETHER TO DIVORCE

The decision to divorce usually is not an easy one. It is common for couples to experience periods of ambivalence when deciding whether to remain married. Ultimately, a couple may base its decision on a combination of logic, intuition, and gut feeling.

Imposing structure on the decision-making process may be helpful. If you are considering divorce, you might benefit from creating a series of lists. The first two lists could enumerate reasons for staying married and reasons to divorce. Such reasons might include: things you like and don't like about your spouse; the potential impact of divorce on your children; potential impact on your relationships with extended family and friends; financial security; and the day-to-day needs and services provided by your spouse.

Note that not all items on your lists will have an equal impact on your decision making. If you like approaching issues in a quantitative way, you might try assigning a number value to each item—for example, a value of five for items of high importance, three for items of moderate importance, and one for items of little importance. Add the values of the items in each list, then see how the numbers compare. Put the lists away for a while, then return to them later to gauge whether other factors have presented themselves, or whether existing items on the lists have become more or less important to you.

You might also benefit from creating a third list, somewhat related to the first two lists, that enumerates a set of goals for your life. Try to list all of your important goals. Such goals might include a warm, sharing relationship with a mate; productive, happy children; time with friends; a satisfying job; financial security; travel; recreational activities; and spiritual growth. Examine your list, and try to determine whether staying with your mate will advance or interfere with your goals—and, conversely, how a divorce might advance or interfere with those goals.

Many couples experience difficult periods in their marriages. During such periods, it is common for one or both partners, after yet another fight or humiliation, to think to themselves, "I can't take this any more! I've got to get out of this relationship!" But while divorce may ultimately prove to be the best option for some couples, it is also important for couples to realize that difficulties are a natural part of many marriages. Indeed, the negative times may simply need to be kept in perspective, as one part of a cycle that will not always prove so difficult.

One way of gaining such perspective is to keep a log or make marks on a calendar to indicate how you feel about various aspects of your life—your spouse, your marriage, yourself, or life in general—at various times. Make brief notations, perhaps in code if you are worried about discovery, indicating how you feel each day. Keep the log for a month or two, and then examine the overall picture. Do the bad days really outnumber the good? Is

THE SECRET DIARY?

One cautionary note about keeping logs or diaries, including those kept on a computer: In some states, such diaries may be subject to **discovery** in a lawsuit—meaning that your spouse and your spouse's attorney may be able to order you to produce your logs, diaries, or e-mails for inspection if they might prove relevant to some issue in the case. In other states, logs and diaries may be protected under a right of privacy or under rules that keep documents you prepare to help your attorney with your case confidential.

there a pattern to the good days or the bad ones? Do the same issues recur day after day?

Ultimately, the decision whether to divorce boils down to the question: "Am I better off with my spouse or without my spouse?" The answer can be found by assessing not only how you feel about your spouse and how your spouse feels about you, but also how every aspect of your life would be different after a divorce. There may be prospects for a better romantic relationship after divorce—but other things will be different, too. Will that total cluster of differences constitute a net improvement or a net deficit?

On the subject of hope for a better relationship in the future, take inventory of the reasons for the breakdown of your current relationship. Try to assess whether you truly have the perspective and skills necessary to build a better relationship next time around.

A complete understanding of what went wrong in a failed marriage is difficult to achieve. It requires some genuine soul-searching, with careful attention to patterns that developed early in each partner's life. Many therapists have noted that people seem to have an unconscious "radar"—an intuition that draws them to mates with significant personality traits resembling those of their parents, particularly negative ones.

Husbands and wives who had conflictual relationships with their parents may have vowed not to marry someone with similar issues. Unfortunately, people often select partners whose personalities duplicate many of the problems with which they were raised. There is comfort—though perhaps unconscious comfort—in things that are familiar, even if the result is conflict.

Before embarking on a new path in the quest to feel whole, it is best to ensure that the path will be a better one. In that regard, consider a study conducted by University of Chicago sociologist Linda Waite and her colleagues. Professor Waite found that two-thirds of people who considered themselves unhappily married, but who nonetheless stayed married, considered themselves happily married five years later. The researchers noted that persons with improved marriages fell into three broad categories. Couples in the largest group simply outlasted their problems. Over time, the sources of conflict or stress in their marriages eased—including financial problems, job reversals, depression, problems with children, and infidelity. Couples in the second group actively worked to solve their problems—by changing behavior, improving communication, or seeking help from clergy or secular counselors. For couples in the third group, the marital problems did not seem to change, but the partners were happier because they had found alternative ways to seek fulfillment despite their mediocre marriages.

There is no precise, automatic formula for deciding whether to divorce. However, many counselors agree that there are certain circumstances in which divorce is often the best solution. For example, divorce may be the best solution if you are married to a person who is abusive; addicted to alcohol, drugs, or gambling; or severely mentally ill. Even in these circumstances, the question exists: "Is your spouse genuinely willing to seek professional help?" If so, your relationship may be worth saving. Your spouse, however, must actually seek help and stick with it; a mere promise to change followed by a few days of improved conduct is not enough.

Describing more subjective factors that affect the decision

whether to divorce, psychiatrist Dr. Peter Martin writes in *The Ann Landers Encyclopedia, A to Z* that "[i]n my experience there are only a few factors that would make a marriage impossible to save. One is the absence in both mates of the ability to feel sympathy for the other. This is usually accompanied by a deep unchanging hatred."

If you do decide to divorce, or if you need to make other changes in your life, monitoring your own well-being may prove beneficial. If you chronically feel sad or if you have low energy, trouble sleeping, or a difficult time focusing on day-to-day tasks, you may be suffering from depression. Similarly, anxieties or phobias about things that did not bother you before, as well as increased frequency of physical illness, are signs of trouble. Seek professional help from a physician or therapist, and evaluate the extent to which your problems are related to your marriage.

For many people contemplating divorce, there is no single, dramatic circumstance that finalizes their decision. For many people, marital problems do not include abuse, addiction, or mental illness. Instead, many partners experience an increasing malaise, coupled with anger—a growing sense that their marriages are not working, and that their relationships are draining more energy than they give back.

For many couples, the primary problem is communication.

This book is not intended as a detailed how-to manual on healing an injured marriage; there are dozens of other books on that subject. However, it is worth recapping some of the most significant advice provided by marriage counselors on how to improve a marriage. Unless the need to leave your marriage is urgent, these steps may be useful:

• Try talking again with your spouse about your feelings. Focus on your feelings and on your partner's feelings. Talk about what makes you happy or sad—what each of you needs. Start with subjects that are relatively noncontroversial, and work up to more sensitive topics.

• Recognize that if you or your spouse come from a family where feelings were suppressed or punished, it may be difficult to talk freely about your feelings. But also recognize that neither one of you is a mind reader. If you want your spouse to understand how you feel and what you'd like, you have to communicate.

• Talk in a way that is non accusatory. Name-calling and enumerating each other's faults simply makes both partners angrier, and usually distracts from the issues that are truly important. Humiliating or demeaning each other is not going to solve your problems.

• If anger erupts, take a time-out: leave the room for a while; take a deep breath; count to ten; hold off further discussion until the next day. Don't respond in anger. But do tell your partner what makes you feel angry or empty.

• In addition to refraining from expressing anger verbally, watch your body language. Sneering or rolling your eyes can have the same counterproductive effect as a verbal assault.

• To help ensure that you each understand what the other is saying, structure your conversations so that you each listen carefully. Allow each partner to speak uninterrupted for a few minutes. After one of you has spoken, have the other repeat the essence of what was said—without commenting on it. The goal at this point is to ensure that each partner understands what the other has said and felt—not to reach agreement on a particular issue.

• Talk about why you feel the way you do. Recall your relationships with parents, siblings, or former spouses. Think about why you may have an emotional "allergy" to certain things your spouse has done or said. Your feelings may seem irrational, but may actually be quite understandable once you and your spouse identify where they come from.

• If you and your partner have fallen into the habit of not spending private time together and communicating, schedule some time. Take a walk; go on a weekend vacation; schedule a series of half hours in the evening when you can spend time together—but not so late in the evening that you are too tired to enjoy them. If you have children, hire a sitter and go out by yourselves. If you can't afford a sitter, perhaps a friend or family member can watch the children for a while.

GOOD COUNSEL

Even if marriage counseling does not save a marriage, a good counselor can facilitate communication and clarify issues. If the marriage is going to end, marriage counseling can be converted into divorce counseling, which can help the parties end the marriage while minimizing harm to themselves and their children.

- Find out what little things would make your partner happy. Do those things, and try to come up with a few other things on your own. Work up to bigger things.
- Marriage counseling can be useful. You can find counselors through a variety of sources, including family physicians, hospital referral services, crisis intervention programs, other community service programs, friends, the Yellow Pages (usually under "Marriage Counselors"), and the Internet. Marriage counseling does not guarantee that a marriage will be saved, but it can help. In order for a marriage to work well, it takes commitment by both partners, and partners who were reasonably compatible in the first place.

IMPACT OF DIVORCE ON SPOUSES

Divorce, of course, is a stressful event in a person's life. Emotional reactions to divorce can include depression, anger, jealousy, humiliation, disorientation, a sense of loss, and denial that the divorce is actually taking place.

Interestingly, many people feel a sense of loss not only with respect to the positive aspects of marriage, but also with respect to its negative aspects. Divorce researchers Andre Derdeyn and Elizabeth Scott have written: "The sense of loss can be just as great if the relationship had long since been almost exclusively negative and conflictual. . . . [T]he intensity of grief is related to the intensity of involvement rather than of love." For many spouses, the marriage—whether dominantly positive or negative—was an integral part of their emotional being, and its loss can be very disruptive.

Judith Wallerstein and Joan Kelly, who have researched the effect of divorce on parents and children, found that the average time required after a divorce for women to reestablish "inner equilibrium," "external stability," and "a sense of continuity in their lives" is three to three and a half years. For men, the average time needed to reestablish continuity was two to two-and-a-half years. In their research, men had a shorter recovery time than women because men, as a group, had more external supports—including greater financial security and job satisfaction—to ease the transition process.

Although most spouses recover from divorce with the passage of time, some do not. Those who do not recover may experience a chronic decline in adult functioning. In many cases, a spouse who is unable to regain equilibrium had his or her primary identity wrapped up in the marriage, and has few inner or external resources on which to fall back.

Often, divorcing parents find that their parenting skills decline during the period of divorce. In the time surrounding a divorce, it is common for parents to become more self-centered and less available to their children as they cope with their own wounds. In most but not all cases, however, parenting skills return to normal after a few years.

REACTION OF CHILDREN TO DIVORCE

Generally, one of a child's first reactions to divorce is fear of abandonment. The child reasons that if one can parent can leave, the other parent might leave as well. The child needs steady reassurance that he or she will not be abandoned. Ideally such reassurance can come from both parents, including through substantial contact with both parents.

Often, young children are also concerned that the parent who is moving out will not be taken care of or will not have a place to stay. Some of these concerns can be alleviated by promptly showing the child where the departing dad or mom will live.

Other common reactions of children to divorce include: sleep disturbances, fears of impending disaster, suspiciousness, underachievement in school, decline in the quality of peer relationships, emotional constriction, anger, and regressive behavior such as bed-wetting.

Many children feel powerless and vulnerable in the period surrounding a divorce. Assuming a child likes both of his or her parents, he or she may want to stop the divorce. Children often blame themselves for the divorce and think that if they had behaved differently, their parents would not be divorcing.

Children need to be told—often many times—that a divorce is not their fault—that dad and mom are not living together because they couldn't get along, and not because the child did something wrong.

Although nothing takes all the pain out of divorce for a child, Dr. Wallerstein notes that the manner in which children are told about a divorce will have a lasting effect on them. Certain ways of telling a child about a divorce can maximize suffering—such as telling the child, "He left *us*!" or "She doesn't love *us*!"

Telling a child that a divorce will not make a difference to his or her life is also unwise. Obviously, the divorce will make a difference. The child should be given a simple, honest explanation of the divorce, without lurid details designed to alienate the child from either parent. Parents should explain what will and will not change in the child's life—including where the child will live, where the child will go to school, and when the child will be with each parent.

The child should be given an opportunity to express feelings and to ask questions. The child also might be told that things will be difficult for a while, but that they will improve with the passage of time.

Studies have shown that one of the most important ingredients for a child's recovery is a close, ongoing relationship with both parents.

PROCEEDING WITH A DIVORCE

As discussed in the opening section of this chapter, the process of deciding whether to divorce can be filled with ambivalence and anxiety. When the decision to divorce is reached, however, it also can be a time of relief.

In their book *Bailing Out* (Fireside Books 1993), which examines the psychological aspects of divorce, Barry Lubetkin and Elena Oumano write:

> 'bailing out' when you know your relationship is no longer viable can be one of the most affirmative, liberating acts of one's life. Bailing out can be a wonderful growth experience *if* you use this period of your life as a time to explore, discover, and evaluate beliefs that have determined your behavior. . . . The irrefutable fact is that staying with someone in a miserable or indifferent relationship, whether in a marriage or a live-in situation, erodes your self esteem.

Ann Landers echoed part of this view in *The Ann Landers Encyclopedia, A to Z:* "Life is too precious to waste years in a joyless marriage—or, worse yet, in a miserable one."

Once you have decided to divorce, or have a strong inclination to do so, a question of timing may remain: When do you announce the decision or take additional steps such as separating or filing a legal action? The answer involves balancing the stresses of maintaining the status quo with the benefits of waiting.

Sometimes it is best to wait. If you are feeling emotionally spent and have no concrete plan as to how to proceed, it may be useful to pause while you muster emotional energy and plan the next phase of your life. Steps to take include: deciding where you want to live; figuring out custody options if you have children; determining whether employment-related changes will be necessary; planning a budget—or, depending on how the divorce proceeds, a range of budgets; consulting with a lawyer; consulting with a therapist or financial advisor if their services are likely to be helpful; and cementing ties with friends, family, and other support networks during your time of transition.

The list of issues on which to work may seem daunting, but when the issues are addressed one step at a time, they can be manageable.

Talking with friends who have gone through a divorce can be helpful. In addition to providing emotional support, friends also can offer perspectives on how to cope with the resulting changes.

Advance planning has psychological advantages. One study found that, for women, the amount of time that elapses between the decision to divorce and marital separation is positively associated with the ability to adjust to divorce. In other words, the longer some people wait to divorce after deciding to do so, the better the adjustment—though adjustment in a short period of time is also possible.

Embarking on a new path is a time for renewal. At some point, most people in unhappy marriages have stopped participating in certain activities that once brought them pleasure, or have failed to pursue other activities that they always wanted to pursue. Now is the chance to pursue those activities. Such new outlets may include a recreational activity, a college course, involvement in religion, theater, more time with friends, or simply quiet evenings spent home alone.

Divorce is a beginning as well as an end.

THE WORLD AT YOUR FINGERTIPS

- The "Can This Marriage Be Saved?" feature of *Ladies' Home Journal,* including back issues and advice by topic, can be accessed online at *www.lhj.com/lhj/.* (Click on "Relationships.")
- For information about marriage and family therapy and assistance in finding a counselor, visit the American Association for Marriage and Family Therapy website at *www.aamft.org.*
- Among the useful books about surviving divorce is *Crazy*

Time: Surviving Divorce & Building a New Life by Abigail Traf-ford, published by HarperCollins.

• Information about depression can be obtained from the National Mental Health Association website at *www.nmha.org/ infoctr/factsheets/21.cfm.*

REMEMBER THIS

• The decision divorce can involve a blend of logic, intuition, and gut feeling. Before deciding to divorce, try to answer a few key questions: (1) is the problem transitory or permanent?; (2) what steps could be taken to make the relationship better?; and (3) when considering the impact of divorce on many areas of your life and on your relationships, will you be better off staying married or getting divorced?

• After a divorce, it is common for both men and women to require two or more years for a sense of inner equilibrium and stability to return. This sense of equilibrium and stability may return more quickly if a person has external supports—including financial security, job satisfaction, and good friends.

CHAPTER 9

Separation, Annulment, and Divorce

Charles and Rachel are considering ending their marriage, but are not sure whether divorce is what they want. They have decided to live apart for a while. They want to know their rights and obligations regarding support, time with children, and use of assets that they acquired during the marriage. What are their options?

Slightly less than half of all marriages in the United States end in divorce. The divorce rate is down from its peak from 1979 to 1981, but the current divorce rate is still near double what it was in the 1950s. (Perhaps if men and women spent more time before marriage exploring issues they will likely face during marriage, the divorce rate would be lower.) Meanwhile, the marriage rate has been dropping since the 1980s—down 30 percent between 1980 and 2004.

As was discussed in Chapter 2, states set requirements for marriage. They also set requirements for ending a marriage—but these regulations are more complicated, since there are more issues to sort out when a marriage ends than when it begins.

SEPARATION AND SEPARATE MAINTENANCE

Separation, as the term implies, means that a wife and husband are living apart. The spouses generally are not required to separate in order to obtain a divorce—though for psychological reasons, it usually works out that way. In some states, certain grounds for divorce may require that the parties live apart for a specified

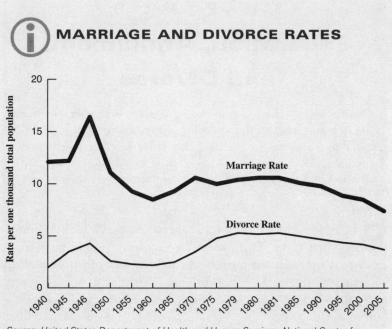

MARRIAGE AND DIVORCE RATES

Source: United States Department of Health and Human Services, National Center for Health Statistics

period of time, but in most states divorce does not require a period of separation.

A **legal separation** also means that a husband and wife are living apart. But in a legal separation, the arrangement is ordered by the court or agreed to by the parties in a written document.

Payments of support during a period of separation sometimes are referred to as **temporary maintenance** or **alimony pendente lite**. ("Pendente lite" is a Latin phrase that means "while the action is pending.") If the person obliged to make such payments fails to do so, a court could order the payments and take steps to enforce that order, by garnishing wages or bank accounts or holding a person in **contempt of court**.

Written agreements regarding support are necessary if the person making the payments wishes to claim a tax deduction for

REASONS TO SEPARATE LEGALLY

The main reason for obtaining a legal separation instead of an informal separation is to make the rights and responsibilities of the parties during the period of separation more certain. If one party—usually the wife—will be receiving financial support during the period of separation, the court order or written agreement will make support an enforceable right.

In some states a Judgment for Legal Separation is allowed; this judgment provides for property, custody, and support similar to a final divorce judgment. However, the parties are not free to remarry. People make this choice for a variety of reasons, including religious principles, continued health care benefits and so on.

paying support. If the person paying support obtains a deduction for the amount paid, then the same amount will be treated as taxable income to the recipient. Without a written agreement or court order, payments of support will not be deductible by the payor, nor will they be treated as income to the recipient. (For more discussion of the tax treatment of support payments, see Chapter 11.)

If a husband and wife have children, the separation agreement or court order can specify arrangements regarding custody, visitation, or parenting time with the children, and those arrangements also can be enforced by the court. A separation agreement also can provide for who will occupy the family home while the divorce is pending, and the degree to which the parties can liquidate or transfer assets, such as funds in an investment account.

An informal or legal separation does not mean that a husband and wife must divorce. They are free to reconcile at any time and resume living together. For some couples, a separation serves as a cooling-off period—a way to relieve immediate pressure while they sort out what they want to do with their lives.

SEPARATION VS DIVORCE

A separation or legal separation is not the same as a divorce. Persons who are separated may not remarry. If they wish to remarry, they must wait until a divorce is final. The terms of a separation agreement usually can be modified by the court or by the parties themselves during the period of separation. Courts, or the husband and wife by agreement, also can modify the provisions of support, custody, and visitation when the divorce is finalized.

If a husband and wife decide to live together again while a court action is pending, the action should be **dismissed**—at least after the spouses are reasonably sure they will stay together. "Dismissed" means that the case has been taken off the list of active cases before the court. If the couple does not dismiss its pending case, the court usually will dismiss it automatically if no action has been taken on the case after a certain period of

TERMS OF SEPARATION

If the final terms of a divorce are likely to be contested, the parties should be cautious about what they accept as a voluntary, temporary arrangement during separation. Although courts usually have the power to depart from the terms of a separation agreement when entering a final order of divorce, judges are likely to examine the separation agreement and think, "If this arrangement was workable during separation, it should work after divorce, too." If someone is agreeing to terms during a period of separation that they would not want to live with after the divorce, they should make abundantly clear in the separation agreement that they are not binding themselves to the same conditions after the divorce is final.

time—usually six months to one year. If the couple later decides to divorce, the case can be refiled.

ANNULMENT

An **annulment** is a court ruling that a supposed marriage was never valid. One of the most common grounds for annulment is fraud. For example, one person may have not disclosed to the other a prior divorce, a criminal record, or an unwillingness to have sexual intercourse. An annulment also may be granted if one of the parties was still married to someone else at the time the supposed marriage took place. Other bases for annulments include marriage to an underage person, marriage to a too-close blood relative, and duress.

Annulments are much less common than divorces because divorces are generally easier to obtain, and the bases for annulment are narrower than the bases for a divorce. One party may prefer an annulment, however, in order to avoid some of the financial obligations that a court might impose in a divorce proceeding. For more discussion of legal annulments, see Chapter 2.

Aside from annulments granted by a court, a person also may seek a religious annulment of a marriage. A few religions will not permit a member of the faith to enter into a marriage if that person has already had one valid marriage. In that circumstance, a divorced person would not be permitted by a member of the clergy of that faith to remarry, since the existence of a divorce implies that a valid marriage already existed. However, if that person was able to obtain a declaration by a religious court or official that the first marriage was not valid, then he or she may be free to remarry.

If a person seeking a divorce or legal annulment is concerned about the ability to remarry within his or her faith, that person should seek an agreement or court order that the former spouse will cooperate in obtaining a religious annulment or divorce.

DIVORCE

A **divorce**—referred to in some states as a **dissolution of marriage**—is a decree by a court that a valid marriage no longer exists. A divorce leaves both parties free to remarry. A **judgment of divorce**—the formal paper issued by the court—usually provides for division of property and makes arrangements for child custody and support, if applicable.

Although divorces may be emotionally contentious, most divorces—probably more than 95 percent—do not end up in a contested trial. Usually the parties negotiate and settle such things as division of property, spousal support, and child custody between themselves, often with an attorney's help. Sometimes parties reach an agreement by mediation, with a trained mediator who tries to help husband and wife identify and accommodate common interests. The parties then present their negotiated or mediated agreement to a judge. Approval of a mediated agreement is virtually automatic if the agreement appears to meet a minimal standard of fairness. Mediation is discussed further in Chapter 16.

If parties are unable to agree about property, support, and child custody, they may ask the court to decide one or more of those issues. Chapters 10 through 13 will discuss in detail how courts decide those issues.

In most states, a threshold requirement for obtaining a divorce is **residency** or **domicile** of one or both parties. "Residency" refers to the state in which a person lives; "domicile" refers to the state the person regards as home. Usually the state of a person's residency and domicile are the same, but sometimes they can be different. For example, a couple may reside in their summer home for four months each year, but regard another state where they spend the rest of the year as their true home. The latter state would be the state of their domicile.

Residency and domicile requirements vary. A few states have no residency requirement, which means that a person can arrive in those states and seek a divorce on the same day. Other states

GROUNDS FOR DIVORCE AND RESIDENCY REQUIREMENTS

STATE	No Fault Sole Ground	No Fault Added to Traditional	Residency or Domicile Requirements
Alabama		x	6 months
Alaska	x	x	6 months
Arizona	x	x	90 days
Arkansas		x	60 days
California	x		6 months
Colorado	x		90 days
Connecticut		x	1 year
Delaware		x	6 months
District of Columbia	x		6 months
Florida	x		6 months
Georgia		x	6 months
Hawaii			6 months
Idaho		x	6 weeks
Illinois		x	90 days
Indiana			60 days
Iowa	x		1 year
Kansas			60 days
Kentucky	x		180 days
Louisiana		x	6 months
Maine		x	6 months
Maryland		x	1 year
Massachusetts		x	None
Michigan	x		6 months
Minnesota	x		180 days
Mississippi		x	6 months
Missouri		x	90 days
Montana	x		90 days
Nebraska	x		1 year
Nevada			6 weeks

New Hampshire	x	1 year
New Jersey	x	1 year
New Mexico	x	6 months
New York	x	1 year
North Carolina	x	6 months
North Dakota	x	6 months
Ohio	x	6 months
Oklahoma		6 months
Oregon	x	6 months
Pennsylvania	x	6 months
Rhode Island	x	1 year
South Carolina	x	3 months (both residents)
South Dakota	x	None
Tennessee	x	6 months
Texas	x	6 months
Utah	x	90 days
Vermont	x	6 months
Virginia	x	6 months
Washington	x	1 year
West Virginia	x	1 year
Wisconsin	x	6 months
Wyoming	x	60 days

This chart appeared in the ABA's publication *Family Law Quarterly*, Vol. 38, No. 4 (Winter 2005), and is reprinted by permission

require residency ranging from six weeks to one year, though six months is the most common requirement. In states with a residency requirement, a party must have lived in that state for the specified period before a divorce can be granted.

The party seeking a divorce must state the grounds for divorce in papers filed with the court. A divorce may be **no-fault** or **fault-based**, depending on the circumstances. All states now offer no-fault divorces, although some states require a long period of separation before a no-fault divorce is granted. Approximately thirty-two states also offer fault-based divorce as an additional option. (See chart above.)

A **no-fault divorce** is a divorce in which neither spouse blames the other for the breakdown of the marriage. There are no accusations necessary to obtain a divorce—no need to prove guilt, or "fault." Common bases for a no-fault divorce include irreconcilable differences, irretrievable breakdown, and incompatibility. In the case of marriages ended on these bases, the court and the legal documents do not try to assign blame.

Another common basis for a no-fault divorce is that the parties have lived separately for a certain period of time, such as for six months or a year, with the intent that the separation be permanent.

Over the last forty years, no-fault divorces have replaced fault-based divorces as the dominant type of divorce. No-fault divorces are widely considered a more humane and realistic way to end a marriage. Husbands and wives who are divorcing usually are suffering enough without adding more fuel to the emotional fires by trying to prove who did what to whom. The laws of no-fault divorce recognize that human relationships are complex, and that it is difficult to prove that a marriage broke down solely as a result of one person's actions.

Some critics of no-fault divorces fear that an economically dependent spouse may not be adequately protected when it is so easy for the other spouse to obtain a divorce. Such critics argue that no-fault divorces result in lower awards of property and support to economically dependent spouses than fault-based divorces. With respect to this issue, however, proof of cause and effect can be difficult to obtain.

In the approximately thirty-two states that also allow fault-based divorces, the grounds for such divorces vary. Possible grounds for fault-based divorce include: adultery, physical cruelty, mental cruelty, attempted murder, desertion, habitual drunkenness, use of addictive drugs, insanity, impotence (usually unknown to the other partner at the time of marriage), and infection of one's spouse with venereal disease.

CHOOSING GROUNDS FOR DIVORCE

Husbands or wives in the mood for revenge probably could come up with multi-count divorce complaints. Some spouses want the emotional release of proving fault on the part of their mates. But courts are not a very good forum for such personal issues, and the accuser usually ends up less satisfied than he or she expected to be. The degree to which fault affects division of property, support, and custody will be discussed in later chapters.

COVENANT MARRIAGES

Legislators in some states have adopted the concept of **covenant marriage**. As of 2005, three states have laws regarding covenant marriage: Arizona, Arkansas, and Louisiana. Louisiana adopted the first covenant marriage law in 1997.

In states with covenant marriage laws, a couple has the choice of obtaining a regular marriage license or a covenant marriage license. With a covenant marriage license, the couple commits to undergo premarital counseling, and commits to seeking counseling before seeking a divorce. In addition, the grounds for divorce are narrower in the case of a covenant marriage than in the case of regular marriage. Depending on state law, the grounds for divorce with a covenant marriage may be restricted to more serious fault-based grounds, such as physical abuse or adultery.

Proponents of covenant marriage see it as a way to strengthen marriage and deter divorce. However, critics fear that covenant marriage laws keep people in conflictual, dysfunctional relationships for longer periods of time, which can be harmful to children as well as to spouses. In the three states with covenant marriage laws, only 1 to 2 percent of people marrying have opted for covenant marriages instead of regular marriages.

RESUMPTION OF UNMARRIED NAME

After divorce, a woman who took her husband's last name during the marriage may either resume her unmarried name or keep her married name. She can even change her name to something completely new, as long as she does not do so for fraudulent purposes. Court proceedings generally are not necessary in order to change one's name.

If a woman is changing her name, she should notify government agencies and private companies that have records of her name—including such institutions as the Internal Revenue Service, Social Security Administration, passport agency (a division of the U.S. State Department), post office, state and local tax agencies, driver's license bureau, voter registration bureau, professional licensing agencies, professional societies, unions, mortgage companies, landlord, banks, credit card companies, telephone companies, cable and other utility companies, magazines and newspapers to which she subscribes, doctors and dentists, and schools and colleges that she attended or that her children attend.

It can be useful for a woman to have her divorce decree state that she will resume her unmarried name, but generally it is not necessary to do so in order for a woman to make a valid name change.

THE WORLD AT YOUR FINGERTIPS

• More information about grounds for divorce can be found at the Divorce Law Center's website at *www.divorcelawinfo.com/Pages/grounds.html*.

• In addition, state-by-state descriptions of divorce law can be obtained from *Divorce Magazine*'s website at *www.divorcemagazine.com*—click on "Divorce Law" and then click on the name of the state in which you are interested.

• Links to the divorce statutes of each state are available through the Legal Information Institute of Cornell University's website at *www.law.cornell.edu/topics/divorce.html*.

REMEMBER THIS

• A legal separation can be an agreement signed by the parties, an order of the court, or both. A legal separation creates legal rights that can be enforced by a court while a divorce is pending. These rights might include child support, alimony, occupancy of the family home, and allocation of time with children.

• All states allow no-fault divorce on such grounds as irreconcilable differences or incompatibility. As an alternative, most but not all states allow fault-based divorce on such grounds as mental cruelty, physical cruelty, and adultery.

CHAPTER 10
Dividing Property

Ted and Alice, both age fifty-five, decide to divorce after twenty-two years of marriage. Their main assets are their house, which is 80 percent paid for, Ted's pension, Alice's IRA, and Alice's investment account, which she inherited from her father. They also have two cars and assorted personal property. They both work outside the home. By what rules will their property be divided?

In the event of a divorce, a husband and wife generally are free to divide their property as they see fit. To facilitate division of property, they may enter into what is called a **marital settlement agreement**. A marital settlement agreement is a contract between a husband and wife that divides property and debts and resolves other issues of a divorce. Although many divorces begin with a high level of acrimony, a substantial majority of divorces—95 percent or more—are settled by a husband and wife, with help from attorneys, without the need for a judge to divide property or decide other issues.

When a husband and wife reach a marital settlement agreement, they can take the agreement to court, where a judge usually will approve it after a short hearing. Some states with simplified divorce procedures might not even require a hearing if the husband and wife agree on everything stated in the agreement.

Settlement agreements operate in what is sometimes referred to as "**the shadow of the law**"—meaning that agreements are influenced by the parties' and their attorneys' awareness of how a judge might decide the case. It may not be possible to predict with complete precision what a judge would do, but an experienced attorney can predict a range of possible results. With those theoretical results in mind, parties often prefer to reach their own agreements rather than go through the monetary and emotional expense of a trial.

DECIDING WHETHER TO GO TO TRIAL

The decision whether to go to trial to have a judge decide contested issues often involves a cost-benefit analysis. If the financial benefit that may result from a trial is high compared to its cost, it may make sense to go to trial. For example, if the parties dispute the value of a business started by the husband during the marriage, and the difference in their valuations is substantial, then it may make sense to let a judge decide the issue rather than submit to unreasonable valuations proposed by one side or the other.

In the example stated above, the parties would need to look at the facts objectively. How much attorney time will it take to develop facts about the business? How much will it cost to hire an expert to evaluate the business and testify at trial? If, after gathering preliminary information and attempting negotiations, the husband still says the business is worth $50,000 and the wife still believes the business is worth $1 million, the only way to solve the problem may be to go to court. (Chapter 16 will discuss mediation and other alternative means of resolving disputes.)

On the other hand, if the business is very small, and the husband says it is worth $15,000 while the wife says it is worth $25,000, it may not make much sense for one or both sides to spend $10,000 in attorneys' fees and experts' fees to ascertain the business's precise value.

NONMARITAL PROPERTY

The laws of dividing property vary from state to state. As a starting point, however, most states allow parties to keep their own **nonmarital property**—also referred to as **separate property**. Nonmarital property includes property that a spouse brought into the marriage and kept separate during the marriage. It also includes inheritances and gifts received and kept separate by one spouse during the marriage. A few states permit division of nonmarital as well as marital property when parties divorce, but the origin of the property is generally considered when deciding who receives it after the divorce.

The right of a spouse to keep his or her nonmarital property may depend on the degree to which the property was, in fact, kept separate during the marriage. For example, if a wife comes into a marriage with a $20,000 money market account and wishes to retain it as nonmarital property, she should keep the account in her own name and not deposit any funds earned during the marriage into the account. She should not, for instance, deposit her paychecks into the account, because the paychecks are marital funds. Depositing them in the account could render the entire account marital property in the eyes of a court. (For a discussion of marital property, see the next section of this chapter.) The process of changing nonmarital property into marital property, and vice versa, is sometimes called **transmutation,** a term that derives from Latin words meaning "cross" and "change."

Another example: During a marriage, if a husband inherits some stock from his mother and wants to keep it as nonmarital property, he should open his own investment account and should not use the account for any investments that he and his wife own together. If a husband or wife decide to use nonmarital funds for a common purpose, such as purchasing a home in joint tenancy, those funds normally will become marital property. The nonmarital property will be viewed by the courts of most states as a gift to the marriage, and thus divisible as the courts see fit in the event of divorce.

Similarly, if a wife or husband takes nonmarital funds and places them in a joint checking account, the funds generally will become marital property. In some states, the presumption that funds placed in a joint account are marital property can be overcome by specific proof that the spouse depositing the funds did not intend to have the funds used for a marital purpose. Nonetheless, if a husband or wife does not want nonmarital property converted into marital property, it is always best to keep the nonmarital property separate.

THE INTRICACIES OF PROPERTY DISTRIBUTION

Property distribution laws have many intricacies and can vary widely by state; understanding them usually requires a lawyer's help. For example, in many states, an increase in the value of nonmarital property—such as an investment account, or a house held in the name of only one party—is considered nonmarital property. In other states, however, this is not the case. You may want to consider hiring an attorney if you need detailed information about property distribution laws in your state.

MARITAL PROPERTY

Marital property—also referred to as **community property,** though subtle differences exist between the two—is defined somewhat differently by different states. Generally, marital property includes property and income acquired during a marriage. Wages earned and homes, furniture, and cars purchased during the marriage are all usually considered marital property.

A court has the power to divide marital or community property between the parties. One party does not have an automatic right to keep marital or community property in the event of a divorce.

Even if title to property is held in the name of only one spouse, the property will not necessarily be considered marital or community property. Assume, for example, that a wife and her husband both work and use their wages to purchase a car. If title to the car is in the name of only one spouse, the car still is marital property because payments for the car came from marital funds—that is, from the couple's wages. Even if one spouse bought the car with his or her wages, was the only driver, and held title to the car, the car still is marital property because payments for the car came from marital funds—that is, from the couple's wages. As a practical matter, if husband and wife own two cars and a judge has to decide who receives which car, each spouse probably would receive the vehicle that he or she primarily drove. Nonetheless, if the property in question is marital property, the judge has the power to give it to either party.

A pension is also usually marital property, even though it may have been earned by the labor of only one spouse during the marriage. To the extent that rights to a pension were earned partially during the marriage and partially before it, the part earned during the marriage may be marital property and the part earned before the marriage may be nonmarital property. (Pensions will be discussed in more detail later in this chapter.)

COMMUNITY PROPERTY

The difference between community property and marital property can be subtle. As noted in Chapter 5 ("Financial Aspects of Marriage"), there are nine community property states: Arizona, California, Idaho, Louisiana, Nevada, New Mexico, Texas, Washington, and Wisconsin, as well as Puerto Rico. In community property states, the joint ownership of property acquired during marriage arises when the property is acquired, regardless of how the title is held. For example, if a husband buys a car with his own wages during a marriage, and holds title to the car in his name only, the car would still be considered the joint property of him and his wife from the time the car was purchased.

In equitable-distribution states (which will be described in more detail in the next section), the joint ownership of property—and the classification of property as "marital"—may not arise until an action for divorce or separation is filed. Whether property is classified as "community" or "marital," the court has the power to divide it between the parties.

In some community property states—for example, California—there is an automatic presumption that community property will be divided equally. In California, lawmakers view marriage as a joint undertaking in which both spouses are presumed to contribute equally to the acquisition and preservation of property. The contributions may be different in nature, but they are treated equally. The wage earner does not receive more property than the homemaker, and vice versa. All marital property is divided fifty-fifty, unless the husband and wife had a premarital agreement stating otherwise. (Premarital agreements, also known as "prenuptial agreements," are discussed in Chapter 1.)

California's approach to community property conserves resources. Husbands and wives do not have to spend time and money arguing about who should get more property, since state law dictates that community property will be divided fifty-fifty. Of course, there still may be issues to dispute, such as: What constitutes community property? And what is the value of a particular piece of community property? (For example, if an actress divorces midway through the production of a film, how should her interest in the film be valued?)

Although California may save resources by declaring an automatic fifty-fifty split, however, this approach deprives courts of the opportunity to fine-tune property divisions to meet the needs of individual cases.

FACTORS CONSIDERED IN DIVIDING PROPERTY

In several community property states and in all equitable-distribution states, courts are allowed to fine-tune property divisions. This may or may not be an advantage in your individual case, depending on the cost of fighting over what constitutes "equitable" and your confidence that judges will make fair decisions regarding property.

"**Equitable distribution**" means that a court divides marital property as it thinks is fair. Like community property states, states applying principles of equitable distribution view marriage as a shared enterprise in which both spouses usually contribute significantly to the acquisition and preservation of property.

Unlike community property states such as California, however, equitable-distribution states are not locked into a fifty-fifty split. The division of property could be fifty-fifty, sixty-forty, or seventy-thirty. Courts could even award all of the marital property to one spouse and none to the other, though such an outcome is very unusual. Courts applying principles of equitable distribution consider a variety of factors, and need not weigh the factors equally. This permits more flexibility and more attention to the financial situation of both spouses after the divorce. However, it also makes the resolution of property issues less predictable.

Here are some factors typically considered by states applying principles of equitable distribution:

(1) **Nonmarital property.** If one spouse has significantly more nonmarital property than the other, courts may give more marital property to the less-wealthy spouse. As noted, courts are not obliged to give equal amounts of property to each spouse, but if the parties have sufficient assets to leave each party in a comfortable situation after the divorce, courts usually will try to do so.

(2) **Earning power.** If one spouse has more earning power than the other, courts may award more marital property to the spouse with less earning power. Courts reason that the party with greater earning power can regain money lost in a divorce more easily than the party with less earning power.

(3) **Who earned the property.** Courts may be inclined to award marital property to the party who worked hard to acquire or maintain it. In dealing with a family business, for example, it is common for a court to award all the interest in that business, or a majority of the interest, to the spouse who operates it. In such circumstances, the court is not only considering who earned the property, but is also seeking to disentangle the husband and wife from each other's future financial affairs. If the value of the business is approximately the same as the value of the family home, it is common for the court to award the business to the spouse who primarily operates it, and award the home to the other spouse.

(4) **Services as a homemaker.** Courts recognize that keeping a home and raising children are hard work, and that one

spouse's work as a homemaker often enables the spouse working outside the home to earn more money. Thus, homemaking services typically factor in favor of the homemaker. Some courts also examine a related concept: whether one spouse impaired his or her earning capacity by working as a homemaker. If a party can show that his or her homemaking resulted in missed opportunities for training or job experience that could have resulted in higher income, courts may award more property to the homemaking spouse.

(5) **Waste.** If one spouse wastes money during the marriage, courts will consider this factor—sometimes known as "**economic fault**"—when dividing marital property, even if they do not consider other kinds of fault. Waste—also known as **dissipation**—could include gambling losses, significant sums of money given to family members (particularly over the protest of the other spouse), and money spent on pursuing romantic relationships outside the marriage. Business losses occasionally are considered waste, but more often are considered an ordinary risk of doing business for which neither spouse should be penalized—particularly if the business deal would have benefited both parties had it gone better. In some states, before waste can be considered as a factor in property division, it must be shown that the waste occurred when the marriage was breaking down—that is, a relatively short time before or after one spouse filed for divorce. In other states, waste or dissipation may be considered regardless of when in the marriage it took place.

(6) **Fault.** In some states, courts may consider noneconomic fault—such as spousal abuse or marital infidelity—when dividing property, but most states do not consider fault relevant to property division. In years past, particularly prior to 1965, divorces were always based on fault: one party needed to show fault by the other in order to obtain a divorce, and fault was an important consideration in dividing property and setting support. The more modern view is that courts should focus primarily on economic factors when dividing property, and pay less attention to who did what to whom. Over time, most courts and legislatures have concluded that it is too difficult—and not

worth the time—to try to sort out all the allegations about transgressions that may have occurred in a marriage.

(7) **Duration of the marriage.** In the case of a long marriage, courts may be inclined to make a larger property award to the spouse with less wealth or earning power. The longer the marriage lasted, the more likely a court is to view the husband and wife as equal partners.

(8) **Age and health of the parties.** If one spouse is ill or is significantly older than the other, courts may be inclined to make a larger property award to that spouse. Courts most often examine this factor in cases involving an older wife whose ability to earn money is diminished by her age and health. However, this factor may also affect men—particularly if a man's age precludes the reasonable assumption that he can re-earn a substantial amount of assets if his wife were awarded a majority of the marital assets. In such a case, an equal division of assets would be more likely.

(9) **Tax consequences.** Courts may consider the tax consequences of property division when making their decisions. For example, suppose the sale of a house or the sale of stock as part of a divorce will necessitate the payment of capital gains tax. A court may be inclined to award extra property to the person who will have to pay that tax, as compensation for the added expense. Conversely, if a property settlement results in a tax benefit, the person receiving the benefit may receive less property as a result. In order for a court to consider tax consequences, such consequences usually must be immediate and specific. Courts generally will not speculate about possible tax consequences that may occur several years in the future.

(10) **Premarital agreements.** A written premarital agreement, assuming it is valid, acts as a trump card in the division of marital property. By entering into a premarital agreement, the wife and husband have waived their rights to have a court consider the usual cluster of factors that determine property division. Instead, the parties have determined in advance how their property should be divided in the event of a divorce. (For more information about premarital agreements, see Chapter 1.)

THE FAMILY HOME

What happens to the family home will depend on the facts of each case. If a wife and husband can agree between themselves on what should happen to their home, the court will virtually always accept their decision. If the wife and husband cannot agree, the court will decide for them.

If the parties own a house, condominium, or cooperative apartment and have children who are still living at home, the law favors giving the house to the spouse who will have primary custody of the children, if it is affordable to do so. This promotes continuity in the lives of the children as well as in the life of the spouse who will live in the house. Of course, courts decide custody on the basis of the best interest of the children and will not award custody to a parent who seeks custody as leverage for the final award of the house.

If the parties cannot afford to keep the house, it may be sold and the proceeds divided, or perhaps given entirely to one party. Proceeds from the sale of a house are usually divided after paying off the mortgage and the costs of the sale—such as commissions to real estate brokers, transfer taxes, and attorney's fees.

In some cases, courts adopt a middle-ground approach: The spouse who has primary custody of the children is granted the right to live in the house for a certain number of years, such as until the youngest child graduates high school. That spouse will then buy out the other spouse's interest, or sell the house and divide the proceeds.

In another variation on this arrangement, one spouse has the right to buy out the other spouse's interest in the home for a fixed period of time, such as thirty days. If the first spouse cannot buy out the other spouse—perhaps because he or she was unable to obtain financing—then the second spouse has an equal period of time in which to buy out the first spouse. If neither spouse is able to buy out the other, then the house will be sold and the proceeds divided between them.

When only one spouse will occupy a house after a divorce, arrangements must be made for payment of expenses related to the house. A common arrangement is for the party living in the house to pay for the mortgage, property taxes, utilities, and routine repairs. If the spouse who is not living in the house retains an interest in the house—such as a right to share in the proceeds when the house is sold at a later date—both parties might share in the costs of major repairs. Major repairs might be defined by the nature of the related expenses—for example, roof repairs or the replacement of appliances—or by the minimum cost of the repairs. For example, any repair costing more than $300 might be considered a major repair.

In some cases, the monetary interest of the spouse not living in the house may be set at a fixed dollar amount. That amount could be adjusted for inflation based on the consumer price index issued by the Bureau of Labor Statistics, a division of the U.S.

 ## LIABILITY FOR MORTGAGE PAYMENTS

When a court or marital settlement agreement awards the entire interest in a house to one spouse and makes that spouse responsible for paying future mortgage payments, the spouse who moves out may still be liable for the mortgage. Banks and other lending institutions are very reluctant to relinquish the security of having more than one person responsible for a loan. Thus, the spouse who moved out still is responsible for the loan in the event the other spouse does not pay the mortgage.

However, the spouse who moves out has a legal remedy under what is known as a "**hold-harmless provision**." Pursuant to such a provision, if the spouse who moves out is obliged to pay a loan that the other spouse was supposed to pay, he or she can sue to collect the value of the loss from the delinquent spouse. Assuming the house has a positive net worth, the court could order the house sold in order to repay the spouse who moved out.

Department of Commerce, or based on the house's percent increase in value from the date of the divorce until the date of sale.

As one example based on percent increase in value, assume that a house is worth $150,000 at the time of a couple's divorce in the year 2000, and that the spouse who moved out was given a $30,000 interest in the house at the time of the divorce. If the house is sold ten years later for $300,000, the spouse who originally received a $30,000 interest would then receive $60,000, since the value of the house doubled between the time of divorce and the time of sale.

FAMILY-OWNED BUSINESSES

As noted earlier in this chapter, courts usually award a family-owned business to the spouse who runs that business. The other spouse may be given other assets in exchange, such as the family home or bank accounts.

The situation is more complicated if both spouses are actively involved with a business. The court may set up an arrangement in which one spouse has the right to buy out the other spouse's interest in the business over time. Alternatively, the spouses could be awarded sequential rights to buy out each other's interests—in other words, one spouse would have the right to buy out the other for a certain period of time, and the other spouse would then have that same right for the same period of time. As with division of the family home, a forced sale might be an option if neither party can buy out the other party, though most courts favor giving the business to just one spouse rather than dissolving an ongoing business.

If the court thinks the parties can continue to work together despite the divorce, the court may allow the status quo to continue, with the husband and wife remaining business partners even though they are no longer marital partners.

Valuation of family businesses can be difficult. By its nature, a **closely held business**—a corporation owned by a few shareholders, shares of which are not traded publicly on a stock ex-

INFORMATION FROM UNHAPPY EMPLOYEES

Another source of information about a closely held business may be a disgruntled former—or even current—employee of the business. An employee unhappy with the boss may be willing to pass on information about how much money a business really makes, and what its expenses are.

change such as the New York Stock Exchange or NASDAQ— does not have a value that can be readily ascertained by means of a stock exchange. If the business is of sufficient size, it could be worth the parties' efforts to hire experts such as accountants or business consultants to evaluate the business, assuming the value of the business is disputed or uncertain. On the other hand, if the business is very small or clearly does not have a significant positive value, it may not be worth the time and money required to thoroughly evaluate the business.

When trying to ascertain the value of a business, it is helpful to look at financial statements of the business that reflect its assets, liabilities, income, and expenses. Tax returns and checking account records also can provide valuable information— sometimes more accurate than the company's internal financial statements.

Loan applications of the business—or the owner of the business—also may provide highly valuable information. Businesses and individuals may make overly generous statements about income and assets when seeking a loan. Such statements are very useful to the spouse of the business owner when he or she wants to show that the business is worth more than its owner claims during a divorce.

If there has been a recent good-faith offer to buy the business, such an offer constitutes valuable evidence about the business's value. Information about the purchase price of similar businesses can also be useful.

Cash businesses can be particularly hard to value, especially if the owner of such a business tries to hide income. If the stated income of the business owner does not match the amount of money the parties have been spending in recent years, proof of the parties' expenses compared with declared income can help the court infer that the business is worth more than the owner claims.

If the spouse who is not the business owner presents proof about hidden income or inflated expenses, such proof can be the basis for a greater award of other property—and perhaps alimony and child support—to that spouse. When seeking to claim that income is greater than the other party says it is, be alert for other explanations for the added funds. For example, if your spouse has been meeting business and family expenses using loans that have yet to be repaid, the funds from those loans will not be the basis for a larger award of property, alimony, or child support. On the contrary, you may receive a lesser amount of property, alimony, and child support, since your spouse is likely to be saddled with debt that needs to be repaid.

PENSIONS

When a couple divorces, it may focus first on dividing the property that's easy to see: the home, furniture, cars, and so forth. But the property it can't see—the **intangible property**—is also affected by divorce.

For many families, a pension is the largest asset after the family home. Even if a pension is earned solely by the efforts of one spouse, the portion earned during the marriage is still marital property subject to division by the court. (For a discussion of whether pensions constitute nonmarital or marital property, see the "Marital Property" section earlier in this chapter.)

Many courts prefer to give full rights to a pension to the party who earned it, as long as the other party will have a sufficient amount of income and property from other sources.

However, the court is likely to divide rights to the pension if it is one spouse's primary source of income, even if he or she did not earn it. The court can divide the pension between the

TALKING TO A LAWYER

Q. When dividing assets, will courts take into account the value of the goodwill of our family business? It seems to me that goodwill is a large part of the value of our business.

A. Courts often will place a value on the goodwill of a business and then treat that value as an asset to be divided. For example, a business may be deemed to have value beyond its physical assets—buildings, vehicles, supplies, inventory, and accounts receivable. Goodwill can include the reputation of a company and the likelihood that customers or clients will continue to use the business. Depending on state law, goodwill that is subject to division as property in a divorce may or may not include the goodwill of a professional practice, such as that of a lawyer, doctor, or accountant.

> Answer by Professor Jeff Atkinson,
> DePaul University College of Law, Chicago, Illinois

Q. When they divide our property, will courts take into account the fact that my wife has a medical degree?

A. Yes. A few states, such as New York, will place a value on a professional degree. Of course, a court cannot award a degree to a party who did not earn one, but it can place a value on a degree already earned, and use that value as a basis for giving more property of a different nature to the other party. For example, if one party has a medical degree and the other party does not, the party without the degree may receive a larger share of the family home or a pension than he or she would if the other party had not earned a degree.

> Answer by Professor Jeff Atkinson,
> DePaul University College of Law, Chicago, Illinois

spouses by percentage—for example, 60 percent for one spouse and 40 percent for the other—or by giving a fixed cash amount to one spouse with the remainder going to the other spouse.

Federal law regulates the division of pensions. Specifically, the law allows entry of court orders called **qualified domestic relations orders** (**QDROs**). These orders, when properly entered by a court, require the administrator of a pension plan to send pension checks not only to the worker, but also to the worker's former spouse. The court cannot order a pension check to be written before the worker is entitled to the pension, nor can the court change the total amount of the pension that is due. But even if a spouse has not yet retired and is not yet eligible for a pension, the court can direct that when he or she does become eligible, checks must be sent to his or her former spouse.

For example, if a couple divorces after the working spouse has retired, the court may order that pension payments be divided fifty-fifty. If the couple divorces while the working spouse is still employed and accumulating retirement benefits, the court may ascertain the value of the pension as of the divorce date and order that sum to be divided between the parties. When the working spouse later becomes eligible for retirement benefits, the other spouse will then receive pension payments for the portion of the pension earned during the marriage. The working spouse would receive the remainder of the pension, including whatever portion of the pension accumulated after the divorce.

Qualified domestic relations orders can be applied to pensions offered by most private employers. Different types of orders with different types of forms may be required for military pensions or certain types of government pensions, but in most cases the result is the same: with a properly entered court order, the pension will be divided between the spouses.

DIVIDING PERSONAL PROPERTY

Even in contested cases that have to be decided by a judge, most parties manage to decide between themselves how to divide rel-

SOCIAL SECURITY RETIREMENT BENEFITS

A divorced spouse may be eligible to collect Social Security retirement benefits based on the work record of his or her ex-spouse, as long as he or she:

- is sixty-two or older;

- is unmarried;

- was married to the working spouse for at least ten years; and

- is not entitled to other benefits—for example, retirement or disability benefits—that exceed one-half the wage earner's primary benefit amount.

For the divorced spouse of a worker to collect Social Security retirement benefits, the worker needn't be retired and actually drawing benefits. However, the nonworking spouse must be eligible for the benefits.

The impact of divorce on Social Security retirement benefits is very different from its impact on pension benefits. A worker with a pension is eligible for a certain amount of money in benefits. If a court orders those benefits split between the parties, the worker's share will decrease. With Social Security retirement benefits, on the other hand, the fact that a divorced spouse is eligible for such benefits has no effect on the amount to which the worker is entitled. The worker will always collect the same amount—whether he or she has no eligible spouse, one ex-spouse, or four ex-spouses all eligible to collect based on his or her work record.

That's one reason why establishing eligibility for a divorced spouse is normally not difficult. It doesn't require a court appearance or even notification of the worker. It simply requires presentation of appropriate documentation to the Social Security Administration. Such documentation normally includes proof of:

- identity;

- each party's age;

- marriage; and

- divorce. (Note that the divorce must be final; the legal action cannot be a separation or annulment.)

Original documents generally are best, but certified copies are also acceptable.

A divorced spouse also may be eligible for benefits on the account of a deceased wage earner who was eligible for benefits. Requirements are similar to those outlined above, except that the surviving divorced spouse must be at least sixty—*or* at least fifty and disabled, *or* caring for a child who is also eligible to receive benefits on the deceased wage earner's account. The surviving divorced spouse can remarry after age sixty, and after age fifty if he or she is disabled. The amount of the benefit is approximately equal to the wage earner's primary benefit amount. As with retirement benefits, more than one person can collect. Applicants will need the documents outlined above, along with proof of the wage earner's death and, if applicable, their own disability.

atively small items of personal property. Nonetheless, intense emotions can accompany divorce, and many couples may find themselves battling over even the most mundane items—not because they deem them valuable, but simply for the sake of vengeance.

Even couples who are relatively amicable when splitting up usually manage to find a few pieces of property over which to argue. Such property often is not valuable in and of itself, but instead becomes a focus for the frustrations of a failed relationship. Perhaps it is easier to obtain an emotional release from fighting over some object than to focus on the underlying personal issues that cause a marriage to end.

If parties truly cannot resolve a dispute over personal property, a judge can do it for them—but this normally is not a cost-effective way to resolve an issue. If the judge does have to resolve a dispute, he or she will consider the same factors used to divide marital or community property. (See the "Factors Considered in Dividing Property" section earlier in this chapter.) In addition, the judge may consider who acquired the property, who uses the

AMICABLE WAYS TO DIVIDE PROPERTY

If a wife and husband are having a difficult time dividing personal property, they might try some techniques that have been used by other couples.

For example, the spouses could work together to prepare a list of all the property in dispute. One spouse could then divide that list into two separate lists, and allow the other spouse to select one of the two lists. Each spouse would then take as his or her property the items listed on his or her list. Presumably, the spouse who draws up the lists will have an incentive to divide the property equally. This arrangement is a variation on the age-old method that parents use to encourage equal division of treats between children: have one child divide the disputed item, and let the other child choose which piece to take.

Another option is to use a single list of disputed property. Use a coin flip or other fair method to select one spouse, who then chooses the first piece of property. Then the other spouse chooses, and back and forth it goes until all the property is divided. A variation on this approach is to have a series of lists from which the spouses take turns selecting, one list at a time. The lists might be based on the economic or sentimental value of the items included therein.

Another more elaborate approach requires the parties to draw up a list of disputed property, and to agree on the value of each item on the list. The parties then take turns selecting items of property. When either party reaches his or her designated quota—for example, 65 percent of the property based on the agreed-upon values—then the other party receives the rest of the property.

If the husband and wife have enough fun working together on this distribution scheme, they might even consider getting back together.

property, and whether the property has a special connection to the family of one spouse or the other.

PERSONAL INJURY AWARDS

A personal injury damage award is one type of property that a couple sometimes must divide. For example, if a husband or wife is involved in an auto accident for which someone else is at fault, the injured party might receive—or be entitled to receive in the future—a sum of money for damages. When the couple divorces, the question then arises: Who is entitled to the damage award?

States take different approaches to this issue. Some states view the award as separate, or nonmarital, property. Courts in these states reason that only one spouse suffered the injury, and the damage award was designed to make that injured spouse whole. Thus, the entire damage award belongs to the injured party.

In some personal injury lawsuits, there are two damage awards: one for the party who incurred physical injury, and another for the injured party's spouse to compensate him or her for loss of companionship, or **consortium,** as a result of the injury. (The phrase "loss of consortium" refers to loss of sexual relations and, under some definitions, loss of general companionship.) If a state treats damage awards as nonmarital property, each spouse will be entitled to his or her own damage award, but not to any portion of the other partner's award.

Other states treat damage awards as marital or community property—which means that a court in these states can divide a damage award between a husband and wife. The courts reason that the damage award arose from something that occurred during the marriage and originally was to benefit the entire family; therefore, the award should be treated as marital property. In practice, courts in these states are likely to award more of the damage award to the injured party, though they also have the power to allocate some of the award to the other spouse.

Some states take a middle-ground approach that focuses on

LOOKING FOR HIDDEN ASSETS

In addition to the financial records discussed earlier in this section, consider the following areas of inquiry in cases where you suspect the other party of hiding income and assets:

ORIGINAL TAX RETURNS

If you have reason to believe that the tax returns given to you or your attorney are not the actual returns filed with the Internal Revenue Service or state tax department, fill out Form 4506 asking the Internal Revenue Service to send you a copy of the original forms. Your spouse's signature may be required if you did not sign the tax return. A court can require that your spouse provide his or her signature.

CHILDREN'S BANK ACCOUNTS

A child's bank account might serve as a hiding place for assets. A trace on the source of those assets could lead to the discovery of more income and assets. Similarly, joint bank accounts held by a spouse and another relative also could serve as a hiding place for income and assets.

SAFE-DEPOSIT BOXES

Find out, perhaps through court-ordered discovery, whether your spouse has any safe-deposit boxes. Check bank records to determine when your spouse had access to the boxes, and see if the times of access coincide with other significant events, such as the receipt of large amounts of money from a customer, client, or family member.

EXPENSES, PERKS, AND INCOME

The owner of a closely held business often can manipulate expenses, perks, and income to make it appear that he or she has less income or fewer assets than he or she represents. If the income and assets of a business have changed significantly near the time of divorce, further comparisons and inquiries are warranted.

the type of damage award. Many personal injury damage awards, particularly those set by a judge or jury, are divided into parts. Depending on what type of damage award is given, the payment may go to the injured party or to the parties jointly. Payments for medical expenses are likely to go to whichever party will pay the medical bills; payments for pain and suffering are likely to go to the injured party who experienced the pain and suffering; and payments for lost wages may go to both parties, since the wages lost would have benefited them both.

LOTTERY WINNINGS

Ever since a majority of states acquired "lottery fever," a growing number of news stories and court opinions have addressed how lottery winnings are to be divided in the event of divorce. Sometimes the issue arises when one spouse wins a big lottery after a couple separates, but before a divorce becomes final. The spouse who bought the lottery ticket often wants to keep all the winnings for himself or herself, while the other spouse wants a piece of the action.

The rule in most states is that if the winnings came from a lottery ticket purchased during the marriage—even if the parties were separated—the winnings are marital or community property, which means they can be divided between the husband and wife. In some states, however, the winner may keep all of the winnings if the parties had already separated.

ALLOCATION OF DEBTS

In addition to property, most couples also have debts to divide. Sometimes their debts will exceed their assets. The court, or the parties by agreement, will divide whatever property the couple has, and then allocate the responsibility of each party to pay off particular debts. Thus, for example, a wife may be responsible for paying off the MasterCard bill, the husband for paying off the Visa bill, and so on.

If the debts were jointly incurred, both parties remain ultimately responsible for them. If the spouse who was supposed to pay a particular bill does not pay, the creditor can still look to the other spouse to collect the amount due. For example, if during their marriage a husband and wife apply together for a Master-Card, both signing the application and promising to make payments, both are liable to MasterCard, even if only one spouse uses the card.

In this scenario, if a court or settlement agreement requires the wife to pay the MasterCard bill, but she fails to pay and MasterCard then collects from her husband, the husband can sue his wife for the amount paid. Alternatively, he may be able to deduct his loss from future payments owed to his wife, such as alimony, if applicable.

Given the potential for continued joint debts, even after a divorce, it is important to limit your liability for your spouse's debts. Thus, it is best to close joint credit card accounts or other joint accounts as soon as a divorce is pending, unless you have a great deal of faith in your soon-to-be-former spouse. If it is not possible to close an account due to an outstanding

PROTECTING CREDIT CARD INFORMATION

In light of increasing concerns about identity theft, it is best that your full credit card numbers not be a matter of public record—for example, as part of a divorce settlement agreement that is filed with a court. If credit card or other financial accounts are to be mentioned in an agreement, it is best to refer to them only by name—such as "Visa"—and by their last four account numbers.

debt that cannot be paid immediately, it is prudent to notify the creditor that you will not be responsible for any additional debts incurred.

For example, if you are party to an outstanding home equity loan of $10,000, but the loan has an available credit line of $40,000, it probably is best to notify the creditor—both orally and in writing—that the line of credit should not be extended beyond $10,000. Similarly, if one spouse co-signs a business loan for the benefit of the other spouse's business, the spouse who does not own the business should notify the creditor that he or she will not be responsible for any business debts beyond those already incurred.

In most states, one spouse normally will not be responsible for debts of another spouse that are incurred only in that other spouse's name. In many states, however, an exception will be made for debts that are considered family expenses. Examples of family expenses include groceries for the family, children's necessary medical expenses, and children's clothes. If a debt is considered a family expense, both spouses probably are liable for that debt, even if only one of them incurred the debt. Community property states also generally make spouses liable for debts of the other spouse that are incurred during the marriage. (See page 107 for a listing of the nine community property states.)

Educational loans are a common debt. Generally, a court will direct each party to repay his or her own loans for educational expenses. However, if the debts were incurred during the marriage, the court may direct one spouse to repay the other spouse's educational debts.

MODIFYING OR UNDOING A PROPERTY DIVISION

It is very difficult to get out of a property division that has been agreed to by the parties or ordered by the court. Courts favor "done deals," and do not want to encourage the parties to run back to court to litigate their disputes all over again.

In most states, there is a period of time after a court enters its order during which one of the parties can ask the court to reconsider its decision. Such a request may be called a **motion to reconsider** or a **motion to vacate the judgment**. The applicable time period varies by state, but parties often have thirty days from the entry of the court's order to make such a request.

The party seeking reconsideration may argue that the court made a mistake in understanding the facts of the case or applying the law. The party also may claim that new facts have arisen that render the original order unfair. (Generally, the party claiming new facts must have a good reason for not having discovered the facts earlier.) In most cases, courts turn down a party's request for reconsideration. But if a court accepts the party's arguments, it may modify the order or conduct additional hearings.

Fraud and duress are two other bases for seeking modification of a court order or settlement agreement. **Fraud** means that one party has deliberately deceived the other party with respect to a significant matter. For example, if one party to a settlement agreement lies about the amount of his or her assets, and the other party later finds out that a substantial amount of assets was hidden, the court may have grounds for vacating the property settlement and ordering a new distribution of property.

Duress occurs when one party is forced into an agreement by extreme, unfair pressure from the other party. In cases of duress, a court also might vacate an agreement and order a different distribution of property. However, duress is difficult to prove. Most judges assume that parties to a divorce agreement are under some degree of stress. Thus, the level of stress and pressure that a party must demonstrate before a court will allow him or her to back out of a deal is very high.

The time period within which a party may seek to modify an agreement or order on the basis of fraud or duress usually is longer than the analogous time period in cases of mistaken facts or misapplication of the law. The applicable time period varies from state to state, but a period of one year from the time of the order or agreement is common.

If a party does not like a trial court's decision, another way to seek relief is to appeal to a higher court. The first appeal usually is to the state's appellate court, though if the case was decided in a small state or involves an issue of substantial public importance, a direct appeal to the state's supreme court may be possible.

Appeals are expensive—often costing as much as the trial itself. The decision to appeal must be made promptly, often within thirty days of the trial court's decision. If the party seeking to appeal waits longer than is allowed by statute or court rule to file a **notice of appeal,** the right to appeal may be lost. The notice of appeal is a document that lets the trial court, the appellate court, and the opposing party know that an appeal will take place.

More often than not, appeals are unsuccessful. The likelihood of success depends on the facts of the case.

EFFECT OF BANKRUPTCY

Many people who are deeply in debt make the decision to file for bankruptcy. After the appropriate steps have been taken, a bankruptcy court will declare the indebted person to be bankrupt,

SECOND OPINIONS

Before seeking an appeal, a party may wish to seek an outside opinion— from an attorney who has not been connected with the case—regarding the likelihood of the appeal's success. Sometimes the attorney who handled the trial has been so close to the case that he or she cannot be fully objective about the merits of an appeal.

and grant a discharge in bankruptcy. A **discharge in bankruptcy** means that all or a portion of the debts owed no longer have to be paid. However, a property settlement or court judgment in connection with divorce is not dischargeable in bankruptcy.

Until 2005, the federal bankruptcy law required bankruptcy courts to weigh the hardships between the parties to determine whether property settlements should be discharged in a bankruptcy. The debtor had to pay the property settlement to his or her spouse if it appeared that the bankrupt debtor had enough property and income to do so. If the debtor did not have enough money for the basic support of the debtor and his or her dependents, then all or a portion of the debt could be discharged in bankruptcy.

A new federal bankruptcy law, the **Bankruptcy Abuse Prevention and Consumer Protection Act of 2005,** which went into effect on October 17, 2005, changed the law on property settlements. Under the new law, property settlements and judgments cannot be discharged under any section of the law. For example, suppose that divorcing spouses agree that the woman should be allowed to keep the house, and that she will pay her ex-husband $50,000. If she subsequently goes bankrupt, she will still owe her ex-husband $50,000—even is she loses the house.

In addition, a bankruptcy court cannot discharge past-due payments for alimony or child support. A debtor's bankruptcy may be a basis for reducing *future* alimony and child support, but not for reducing or eliminating *past-due* alimony and child support.

THE WORLD AT YOUR FINGERTIPS

- You can obtain more information about dividing property in divorce on the Divorceinfo website at *www.divorceinfo.com.* (Click on "Property Division.")
- State-by-state descriptions of the law on property division are available from DivorceNet at *www.divorcenet.com.*

• Advice about financial planning in connection with divorce is available at *http://financialplan.about.com/cs/divorceandmoney/a/DivorceIssues.htm*.

• You can find more information about the new bankruptcy law in the ABA Guide to Credit and Bankruptcy (2006), available for purchase online at *www.abanet.org/publiced/practical/books*.

REMEMBER THIS

• In most states, when a husband and wife divorce, they are entitled to keep their own separate, or nonmarital, property. Nonmarital property includes property owned by each spouse before the marriage, as well as property received by inheritance during the marriage, as long as the property is kept separate—for example, in an account in the name of the spouse who received the property.

• Unless a premarital agreement provides otherwise, property acquired during a marriage—including wages and pensions—is considered marital or community property. A court can divide marital or community property as the court thinks is equitable, considering a variety of factors—though in some community property states such as California, community property automatically will be divided fifty-fifty.

• In addition to property, most couples also have debts to divide. The court, or the parties by agreement, will divide whatever property the couple has, and then allocate the responsibility of each party to pay off particular debts.

• Before deciding to go to trial and have a judge decide how to divide property, spouses should undertake a cost-benefit analysis to make sure that the cost of going to trial—including the cost of attorney's fees and expert's fees—will not exceed the potential benefits of a trial.

CHAPTER 11
Alimony/Maintenance

Joshua, age forty-eight, and Ellen, age forty-six, were married for twenty-two years before deciding to divorce. Ellen spent most of the marriage at home raising their children, though she began working part-time as a teacher five years ago. They own a house and have $100,000 in investments. Joshua earns $80,000 per year; Ellen earns $20,000 per year. Should Ellen be able to receive alimony—and, if so, should the alimony be temporary or permanent?

Alimony is a term that refers to payments from one spouse to the other, for the benefit of the spouse who is receiving payment. Some states use the term "alimony"; other states use the terms **maintenance** or **spousal support;** each term means the same thing. (For simplification in the rest of this section, we will use only the term "alimony"; but wherever "alimony" is used, "maintenance" or "spousal support" could be substituted.)

The overwhelming majority of alimony payments are made from husband to wife, but in appropriate circumstances—such as when a husband takes care of the children and home while the wife works outside the home—courts also may order payments from wife to husband. The Supreme Court has held that it is unconstitutional for a state statute to allow alimony payments only to wives; payments to husbands must also be permissible. All states allow courts to order alimony, although some states are more reluctant to order alimony than others.

There are several types of alimony, each of which is designed to meet particular needs.

TEMPORARY ALIMONY

Temporary alimony, or **alimony pendente lite,** is alimony paid when the parties are separated but the divorce is not final.

("Pendente lite" is a Latin phrase that means "while the action is pending.") Alimony may be continued under a different label after the divorce is final, but it need not be.

REHABILITATIVE ALIMONY

Rehabilitative alimony refers to alimony given so that a spouse may rehabilitate herself or himself—that is, acquire greater earning power or training in order to become self-supporting. Rehabilitative alimony also might be paid to a parent who is staying home with young children until such time as it is considered appropriate for him or her to work outside the home.

There is no uniform time at which parents are automatically expected to work outside the home, but many parents resume work after their youngest child starts school full-time. Of course, in many families—both intact and divorced—parents work outside the home even when their children are preschoolers. And in some families, one parent stays home as long as the children live at home. Obviously, circumstances will vary from family to family.

Rehabilitative alimony usually lasts for a fixed period of time. The court, or the parties by agreement, may provide that the alimony is subject to **review** at the end of that fixed period. If alimony is subject to review, the court may examine the facts of the case at a later time to determine whether the alimony arrangement should be continued, discontinued, or altered.

If an order or agreement does not provide for review, alimony may or may not be reviewable, depending on state law. If the recipient of alimony wants the alimony to be reviewable with the possibility of continuation, it is best to include language to that effect in the order or agreement. If the person paying alimony—the payor—does not want alimony to be continued beyond a certain time, then he or she should seek to include language to that effect in the agreement or order. A court is likely to approve cessation of alimony on a certain date if the agreement or order calls for it, but the court usually has the power to continue alimony in certain circumstances, such as chronic illness of the recipient.

PERMANENT ALIMONY

Permanent alimony continues indefinitely. The main bases for ceasing payments of permanent alimony are death of the payor, death of the recipient, or remarriage of the recipient. Cohabitation of the recipient with another person—particularly a member of the opposite sex—also is a common basis for cessation of permanent alimony. Generally, such cohabitation must be of a permanent or near-permanent nature, with the cohabitating parties sharing living expenses. A few overnight visits usually do not constitute cohabitation for the purpose of stopping alimony payments.

Unless an agreement between the parties indicates otherwise, payments of permanent alimony can be adjusted upwards or downwards based on a change of circumstances. For example, if the recipient begins a well-paying job or receives a significant amount of money from another source, such change might be a basis for reducing alimony payments. Conversely, if the recipient incurs unexpected medical expenses that are not covered by insurance, such change might be a basis for increasing alimony payments—if the spouse paying alimony has the ability to pay more.

A decrease in the payor's income, including at retirement, also can be a basis for reducing alimony. Courts may examine the reason for the decrease. If the decrease is not the fault of the payor, the court is more likely to approve a reduction in alimony. If the drop in income seems to have been engineered by the payor to create a basis for reducing alimony, the court is more likely to disapprove a reduction.

REIMBURSEMENT ALIMONY

Reimbursement alimony, as its name implies, is designed to reimburse one spouse for expenses incurred by the other. For example, if one spouse helps put the other spouse through college or a training program, and the couple divorces soon after that program is complete, the spouse who supported the family during the program might be able to obtain reimbursement alimony as payback for the resources spent.

A classic example involves a nurse who marries a medical student and supports the family while the student finishes medical school—and perhaps a residency program. If the couple divorces soon after the medical student completes training, the nurse probably will be entitled to reimbursement alimony to compensate her for the money she spent supporting the family during the student's training. Although most states do not consider a medical degree to be property, the nurse may nonetheless be entitled to monetary reimbursement. In this case, reimbursement alimony is not necessarily awarded because the nurse needs funds for day-to-day support; indeed, the nurse has her own job, and is self-supporting. Instead, the alimony is given as equitable payback for supporting the spouse throughout medical school.

Alternatively, a court could choose to give the supporting spouse a substantial majority of marital property as compensation. But in many cases in which one spouse has completed a training program, the couple has not accumulated a large amount of marital assets. Reimbursement alimony thus provides an alternative, in part because it can be paid over a period of time.

LUMP-SUM ALIMONY

Lump-sum alimony, or **alimony in gross,** is alimony in the form of a fixed payment. Generally, lump-sum alimony is paid even in circumstances where other types of alimony would have been terminated. For example, lump-sum alimony normally is paid even if the recipient remarries. Depending on the wording of the agreement or court order, payments also could be made to the estate of the recipient in the event the recipient dies.

Lump-sum alimony usually is paid in lieu of a property settlement. Depending on how the alimony is structured, it could provide a tax advantage to the payor (see sidebar below). Lump-sum alimony also can serve as a type of reimbursement to ensure that one spouse is paid back for certain expenditures—even if the recipient remarries, cohabits with someone, or does not otherwise need the alimony for day-to-day support.

FACTORS CONSIDERED
IN ORDERING ALIMONY

The criteria for ordering different types of alimony have already been discussed in part. Courts may, however, consider additional

 TAX ASPECTS OF ALIMONY

Alimony usually is treated as income to the recipient and as a deduction from income for the payor. This may result in savings on the couple's combined income tax payments. The reason is that, if one spouse earns less than the other, additional income (in the form of alimony) will be taxed at a lower rate than if the same amount were treated as income to the higher-earning spouse.

Assume a husband and wife are about to be divorced. Before payment of alimony, the wife has a taxable income of $10,000 and the husband has a taxable income of $70,000. If each were to pay taxes on his or her income, their combined tax liability would be $15,179. (Applying 2006 federal tax rates for single filers, the husband would pay $14,057 and the wife would pay $1,122.)

If the husband were to pay the wife $20,000 per year in alimony, his taxable income would drop to $50,000, and the wife's taxable income would increase to $30,000. Their combined federal income tax payments then would drop to $13,179—$9,057 for the husband and $4,122 for the wife. Their combined tax bills would be $2,000 less than if the alimony payments were taxable to the husband.

The wife's tax bills have gone up, but so has her income.

factors similar to those that apply in the context of property division. (For a detailed discussion of these factors, see pages 108–111 of Chapter 10.)

Income and Property of Each Party

The greater the income and property of a divorced spouse, the less likely it is that the spouse will need alimony. Conversely, the less income and property a spouse has, the more she or he will need alimony.

Payment of alimony also depends on the ability of one spouse to pay. Alimony is most likely to be awarded when one spouse has substantially more property and income than the other. If the spouses' levels of property and income are similar, alimony is less likely to be paid. Courts will take into account the division of property that will occur in connection with the divorce. Some courts may order a larger share of property to the less-prosperous spouse in order to avoid or reduce that spouse's need for alimony.

Earning Capacity of Each Spouse

A related factor in the decision whether to award alimony is the present and future earning capacity of each spouse. Alimony is likely to be awarded in a situation where one spouse's earning capacity is much larger than the other's. To the extent that the earning capacity of the less-prosperous spouse would increase if he or she pursued additional training, a court may award rehabilitative maintenance to facilitate such training.

Impairments in Earning Capacity

Courts are likely to award permanent alimony to a spouse with little or no earning capacity—as, for example, in the case of advanced age or chronic illness. Courts also will take into account any limitations on a spouse's earning capacity due to years spent working as a homemaker. Often, spouses who are homemakers delay or give up the opportunity for training or building job skills that could produce a higher income. Meanwhile, in many cases, their spouses are able to work and increase earning capacity, in part because one spouse manages the home. In such circumstances, some courts will grant permanent alimony to compensate for the difference in the spouses' earning capacities.

Children at Home

The presence of young children at home makes courts more likely to grant alimony, at least until the children are in school full-time. Even after the children are in school, the court may grant alimony so that the parent who cares for them need only work part-time. This is more likely to occur if, during the marriage, one parent had been serving as a full-time homemaker. If both parents had been working outside the home during the marriage, the court is more likely to expect a continuation of the status quo. (The U.S. Bureau of Labor Statistics reports that more than 60 percent of mothers with children under the age of three work outside the home.) As with all types of alimony, a key factor is the ability of the more-prosperous spouse to pay. If the better-off spouse has only moderate income, alimony probably will not be ordered or the amount ordered will be modest.

Standard of Living During the Marriage

You may have heard the old-fashioned phrase, often bandied about in connection with divorces, that "a wife is entitled to be supported in the style to which she has grown accustomed." One does not hear that phrase so much any more, but a couple's standard of living during their marriage is still a factor that courts will consider when setting alimony. If possible, the court may grant sufficient alimony and property for the parties to continue the same lifestyle as they enjoyed when they were married. But the reality in most cases is that the money will not go as far as it did during the marriage, since it costs more to support two households than one. If the couple's comfortable lifestyle during the marriage was supported in part by incurring debt, the court will not expect one party to continue incurring debt to support the other.

Because a couple's standard of living is a factor in determining alimony, it is to the advantage of the party seeking alimony to present testimony and exhibits reflecting a prosperous lifestyle. Such exhibits might include pictures or videos of the family home, possessions, and vacations, perhaps accompanied by copies of receipts and checking account records reflecting the level of the family's expenditures.

Duration of the Marriage

The longer a marriage lasted, the more likely a court is to grant alimony, particularly if there is a significant difference between the earning capacities of the parties. Courts are less likely to grant alimony in the case of short-term marriages, unless there are young children at home or the spouse is seriously ill and unable to work for meaningful wages. Alimony normally will not be granted for a time period that exceeds the length of the marriage—though such an arrangement may be ordered if, for example, the person seeking support is chronically disabled.

Contributions of the Spouse Seeking Support to the Education or Career of the Other Spouse

As was discussed earlier with respect to reimbursement alimony (see page 134), courts may grant alimony to a spouse who helps put the other spouse through school or a training program, even if the alimony is not necessary for the recipient's day-to-day support. Similarly, courts may be willing to grant alimony to spouses who actively support their partners' careers, such as through frequent entertaining or through working for no wages in the family business.

Tax Consequences of Property Division and Alimony

Courts may be more likely to award alimony if the payor receives a tax benefit as a result of the way property was divided in the divorce. Conversely, courts may be less likely to award alimony if the payor of alimony must pay additional taxes because of the property division.

Alimony generally is deductible by the spouse who pays it, and is treated as income of the spouse who receives it, unless the parties agree otherwise. Note that if a husband and wife are in different income brackets, the tax treatment of alimony results in a net savings on their combined tax bills. The amount of money the payor saves in taxes by deducting alimony from taxable income is greater than the amount of additional taxes the recipient pays on the alimony, which is treated as taxable income. (See "Tax Aspects of Alimony" sidebar on p. 135.)

Fault

In nearly half the states, fault is not a factor in deciding whether or not to grant alimony (see chart on p. 141). In those states, the legislatures and courts wish to focus on economic factors in deciding who receives alimony and how much they receive. As with property division in these states, courts do not want to embroil themselves in questions of who did what to whom. Thus, if one spouse had an affair, that fact will not affect the granting of alimony.

In approximately thirty states, however, fault is a factor in deciding whether to grant alimony. In some of those states, proof of fault by the spouse seeking alimony completely blocks that spouse's claim. In other states, fault is a factor that can be considered, though the presence of fault by the spouse seeking alimony does not necessarily preclude the entire claim.

Premarital Agreements

As with division of property, a valid premarital agreement—also known as a "prenuptial agreement"—acts as a trump card in determining the level of alimony to be paid in the event of divorce. Through the premarital agreement, the parties have waived their rights to have alimony determined by the usual rules of the court. (For a detailed discussion of premarital agreements, see Chapter 1.) In many states, however, a premarital agreement that provides no alimony or very low alimony to the less-wealthy spouse will not be honored if doing so would leave him or her with no reasonable means of support. In that circumstance, the spouse who lacks capacity for self-support is likely to be granted some alimony.

WHEN SHOULD ALIMONY BE PERMANENT?

A wife and husband, both fifty years old, were married for twenty-nine years. During the first three years of the marriage, the wife worked as a high school physical education teacher. The parties then had four children, and the wife left her full-time job to take care of the home and children for twenty-five years. The husband worked continuously during the marriage, and, at the time of divorce, was an administrator for a charitable organization, earning $77,000 per year. The wife had resumed teaching and her salary was $30,000 per year. Her salary would have been significantly higher, and she would have had substantial retirement benefits, had she continued teaching full-time during the marriage.

In a case based on these facts, the Illinois Appellate Court held that the wife was entitled to permanent maintenance (alimony) in the amount of $600 per month. The court said:

> Marriage is a partnership, not only morally, but financially. Spouses are coequals, and homemaker services must be recognized as significant when the economic incidents of divorce are determined. The [wife] should not be penalized for having performed her assignment under the agreed-upon division of labor within the family.

Source: In re Marriage of Drury *(Illinois Appellate Court, 2000).*

ⓘ CONSIDERATION OF FAULT IN SETTING ALIMONY

STATE	Marital Fault Not Considered	STATE	Marital Fault Not Considered
Alabama		Missouri	
Alaska	x	Montana	x
Arizona	x	Nebraska	x
Arkansas	x	Nevada	x
California	x	New Hampshire	
Colorado	x	New Jersey	x
Connecticut		New Mexico	x
Delaware	x	New York	
District of		North Carolina	
Columbia	x	North Dakota	
Florida		Ohio	x
Georgia		Oklahoma	x
Hawaii	x	Oregon	x
Idaho		Pennsylvania	
Illinois	x	Rhode Island	
Indiana	x	South Carolina	
Iowa	x	South Dakota	
Kansas	x	Tennessee	
Kentucky	x	Texas	
Louisiana		Utah	
Maine	x	Vermont	x
Maryland		Virginia	
Massachusetts		Washington	x
Michigan		West Virginia	
Minnesota	x	Wisconsin	x
Mississippi		Wyoming	

This chart appeared in the ABA's publication *Family Law Quarterly*, Vol. 38, No. 4 (Winter 2005), and is reprinted by permission

LIFE INSURANCE
THAT GUARANTEES ALIMONY

The recipient of alimony may wish to seek an agreement or court order to guarantee support in the event of the payor's death. The usual method of guaranteeing support requires the payor to maintain an insurance policy on his or her life, with the recipient as beneficiary. The amount of the policy should be high enough to compensate for the loss of alimony payments.

In order to ensure that the insurance policy remains in effect, the recipient may seek to require the payor to provide periodic proof that the policy is still in force. This could be accomplished by having the payor provide an annual copy of the policy showing full payment of premiums for the coming year. The recipient also may seek to include a provision in the policy requiring the insurance company to notify him or her in the event that payments are not made on time. As an alternative to an insurance policy, the parties might agree that the payor will post a bond, or that the payor will leave the recipient a certain amount of money by will or by trust in order to ensure continued support.

HEALTH INSURANCE

Direct payment of a former spouse's health insurance premiums normally is not part of an alimony agreement or order, though the recipient certainly may wish to use some of the alimony payments to purchase health insurance if he or she is not already covered.

When a couple divorces, the family health insurance policy—if any—will no longer cover both spouses. The policy will only cover the spouse who purchased the policy or who acquired the insurance through work. Children covered under a family policy generally will still be covered after a divorce.

A federal law passed in 1986—the Consolidated Omnibus

Budget Reconciliation Act, also known as "COBRA"—requires most employer-sponsored group health plans to offer divorced spouses of covered workers continued coverage at group rates for eighteen months after a divorce, and up to thirty-six months in some circumstances. The worker's divorced spouse must pay for the coverage, but the coverage is nonetheless available.

A divorced spouse who wishes to take advantage of COBRA should act as soon as the divorce is final or coverage is lost. He or she should contact the human resources or personnel department of the covered worker's employer to learn the steps that must be taken. Generally, the divorced spouse must act within sixty days of the divorce or loss of coverage; continued coverage is not automatic. The law provides that the worker's employer must explain the divorced spouse's right to continue coverage within fourteen days of being notified, after which the spouse has no more than sixty days to choose to continue coverage. The employer must advise what coverage is available, its cost, and when payments must be made, as well as any steps that must be taken to establish eligibility for the health insurance.

THE WORLD AT YOUR FINGERTIPS

• For more information about laws governing alimony, and other aspects of divorce law including state-by-state descriptions, visit DivorceNet at *www.divorcenet.com.*

• For information about rights to continue health insurance coverage under the federal COBRA law, visit the U.S. Department of Labor website at *www.dol.gov/dol/topic/health-plans/cobra.htm.*

REMEMBER THIS

• Alimony can be awarded for different time periods and for different purposes, including:

- temporary or rehabilitative alimony to facilitate transition and to give the recipient an opportunity to improve her or his economic condition;
- permanent alimony to provide indefinite support, especially if the recipient is never likely to be self-supporting or earn an income approaching the spouse's income; and
- reimbursement alimony to pay back money expended to help the other spouse, such as by putting the spouse through professional school or a training program.

- A court considers several factors in ordering alimony, including:
  - income, property, and earning capacity of each party;
  - standard of living during the marriage; and
  - duration of the marriage.

CHAPTER 12

Child Support

Bob and Mary decide to divorce and share joint custody of their children—a girl, age twelve, and a boy, age five. Both parents work outside the home. Bob earns $60,000 per year, and Mary earns $25,000 per year. The younger child is in an after-school day care program, and both children go to summer camp. How will child support be determined, and who will be responsible for college expenses if the children go to college?

The starting point for determining child support is the set of **guidelines** that have been established by state legislatures or courts. Under federal laws passed in the 1980s, states must establish guidelines for determining child support. Such guidelines were required because the federal government believed that the amounts ordered for child support historically had been too low, and that there was too little uniformity in the process—a fact that often resulted in dissimilar awards for children in similar circumstances.

Establishment of child support guidelines generally resulted in the desired effect: child support payments increased by approximately 50 percent, and support payments within each state became more uniform.

Guidelines are formulas that take into account the income of parents, the number of children in a home, and perhaps additional factors. The formulas are based on studies of how much families ordinarily spend to raise children.

The aim of guidelines is to calculate support payments that are commensurate with what would have been spent supporting a child if the family had not been divided by divorce. Courts plug numbers into the applicable formula, and come up with an amount of support that should be paid for the child or children. The guidelines apply equally to children born to married parents and children born out of wedlock.

REACHING AN AGREEMENT

The parties may make agreements concerning the payment of child support; however, it is a good idea to ask a court to approve the agreement. Some states will not recognize or enforce agreements on child support that have not been approved by a court.

Parents can argue that because of special circumstances, a court should order more or less support than the guideline amount. (For a list of factors that might warrant departure from the guidelines, see the sidebar on pages 150–151.)

DETERMINING PARENTS' INCOMES

When applying guidelines, most states look to either the parents' net income or gross income. **Gross income** is usually defined as the parents' income from all sources, including wages and investments, with no deductions for taxes or other expenses. Nonwage benefits a parent receives from an employer might be counted as income. For example, military housing allowances usually are counted as income when determining child support. If a company car is used for personal business, the value of that use might also be counted as income.

Net income is the parents' gross income minus federal and state income taxes, Social Security tax, Medicare tax, and health insurance costs. Some states will allow other deductions when determining net income. Additional deductions might include: union dues, mandatory retirement contributions, obligations of support to other families, and payment on debts incurred during the marriage that were incurred for the benefit of the family.

For self-employed persons, the determination of income may be complex. Courts will allow deductions of reasonable business expenses before determining net income. But courts may disallow unusually high business expenses and depreciation that reduces income artificially without hurting the parent's cash flow.

Thus, certain expenses that are deductible for tax purposes may not be deductible from income for the purpose of setting child support. For example, if a self-employed parent claims a large deduction for depreciation of office equipment, the deduction may be quite permissible for the Internal Revenue Service. However, it might not be treated as a full deduction from income for the purpose of setting child support, particularly if the office equipment will have a useful life for longer than the time over which the deduction is taken.

EXAMPLES OF GUIDELINES

The amount of money a parent will have to pay in child support varies from state to state, because each state has its own guidelines and judges may differ in their willingness to depart from guidelines.

Generally, there are two types of child support guidelines. One type is based on the income of the person who is supposed to pay child support (the **obligor**) and the number of children. The other type of guideline is based on the income of *both* parents and the number of children. This second type of guideline often is referred to as the **income shares model**.

Child Support Guidelines Based on Percentage of Obligor's Income

Illinois and New York are examples of states with guidelines based on a percentage of the noncustodial parent's income. (New York's guidelines make reference to a percentage of the income of both parents, but for practical purposes child support payments are paid by the noncustodial parent to the custodial parent, since the custodial parent is assumed to spend money for the child without a specific transfer of money that is monitored by the court or the other party.) These were the guidelines in effect in 2005:

Number of Children	Percentage of noncustodial parent's income devoted to child support	
	Illinois	New York
1	20%	17%
2	28%	25%
3	32%	29%
4	40%	31%
5	45%	No less than 35% for five or more children; no less than 50% for six or more children

States use different methods of calculating a parent's income for the purpose of determining child support. Illinois uses "net income," which is defined as income from all sources minus the following deductions: federal and state income taxes (properly calculated); Social Security (FICA) payments; mandatory retirement contributions; union dues; health insurance; payment of maintenance (alimony); payment of other child support obligations; and repayment of certain debts. New York uses "gross income," which is defined as income from all sources minus: certain business expenses; payment of alimony; payment of other child support obligations; public assistance; supplemental security income; Social Security (FICA) payments; and New York City or Yonkers income taxes. (In New York, federal and state income taxes are not deducted before determining a parent's income for the purpose of setting child support.)

Under these guidelines, if a noncustodial parent in Illinois has a net income of $50,000, the annual level of child support would be $10,000 for one child; $14,000 for two children; $16,000 for three children, and so on. In New York, a noncustodial parent with a gross income of $50,000 would pay $8,500 for one child; $12,500 for two children; $14,500 for three children, and so on.

The Income Shares Model

The income shares model, which takes into account the income of both parents, also varies slightly by state. Under one approach, the court first adds the net income (or gross income) of both parents. Then the court consults a long table (or computer program) that assesses the total obligation of support as a percentage of the parents' combined incomes and the number of children. Generally, the percentage of income that must be devoted to support drops as combined incomes rise, on the assumption that affluent parents need to spend a smaller portion of their incomes on their children than parents who are less affluent.

A court applying the income shares model multiplies the parents' combined incomes by the applicable percent figure and obtains a dollar amount that the child or children are considered to need for support. The responsibility to pay that support is then divided between the parents in proportion to each parent's income.

Under another approach, the obligation of each parent is determined by applying each parent's individual income to the child support table or formula to determine their individual obligations of support.

If one parent has primary custody of the children, the other will probably make a cash payment to that parent. The parent with primary custody probably will not make a cash payment as such, but would be presumed to spend the appropriate fraction of his or her income on the children. Alternatively, the parents might set up a checking account for the children's expenses, deposit their respective shares into the account, and agree on the type of expenses that could be paid from the account.

If the parents share equal time (or close to equal time) with the children, adjustments might be made to the formula.

DEPARTING FROM SUPPORT GUIDELINES

The specificity of child support guidelines varies from state to state. Some guidelines are quite detailed and take many factors into account. Courts usually do not depart from such guidelines except in exceptional cases. Other guidelines are more general—providing a certain amount of support based on the income of the parent (or parents) and the number of children, but not taking into account a variety of factors that could serve as a basis for increasing or decreasing the amount of support. Here are some factors that *might* provide a basis for departing from guidelines:

REASONS FOR AWARDING ADDITIONAL SUPPORT

- Child care expenses (especially if unusually high)
- Cost of health and dental insurance
- Medical and dental expenses not covered by insurance
- Cost of special educational needs, such as private school, tutoring, or speech therapy
- Cost of recreational activities such as summer camp, sports teams, and after-school activities
- Income of noncustodial parent's new spouse, which may enable the noncustodial parent to pay additional child support
- Voluntary unemployment or underemployment of the noncustodial parent (in which case the court may attribute to the noncustodial parent income the court thinks that parent should be earning, even if he or she is not actually earning it)

REASONS FOR AWARDING LESS SUPPORT

- Unusual custody arrangements such as splitting custody of the children—in other words, some children live with their mother, some with their father

- Joint or shared custody arrangements in which a child spends an equal or substantial amount of time with each parent

- High transportation costs for a child to visit the noncustodial parent, as when the parents live in different states

- High income of the noncustodial parent, particularly if the guidelines do not have a cutoff point beyond which the guidelines do not apply

- Duty of the noncustodial parent to support other families, including a new spouse and child

- Debts of the noncustodial parent, particularly if the debts were incurred during the marriage to the custodial parent who is seeking support

- Income of the custodial parent's current spouse, which may enable the custodial parent to provide additional child support

- A need to channel funds to a closely held business, which may help the business grow and provide funds for more child support in the future

- Property division in connection with a divorce, such as an award to the custodial parent of a home with a low or paid-off mortgage

- Significant income of the child, as from a trust fund received by inheritance

 CHILD SUPPORT GUIDELINES BY STATE

This chart appeared in the ABA's *Family Law Quarterly* (Winter 2005) and is reprinted by permission. Symbols indicate the following:

   a = mandatory add-ons

   m = mandatory deduction

   p = permissive deduction

   d = deviation factor

State	Income Share	Percent of Income	Extraordinary Medical Deduction	Child Care Deduction	College Support	Shared Parenting Time Offset
Alabama	x	x[3]	x p	x m	x	
Alaska		x	x m	x	x	x
Arizona	x		x m	x p		
Arkansas		x	x d	x d		
California	x		x m	x m		x
Colorado	x		x m	x m		x
Connecticut	x		x d		x	
Delaware			x m	x m		x
District of Columbia		x	x	x	x	x
Florida	x		x p	x m		
Georgia		x	x p	x m		
Hawaii	x	x[3]	x m	x	x	x
Idaho	x		x m	x p		x
Illinois		x			x	
Indiana	x		x p	x m	x	x
Iowa		x		xm	x	x
Kansas	x			x m		x
Kentucky	x		x m	x p		
Louisiana	x		x m	x m		
Maine	x		x m	x m		
Maryland	x		x m	x m		x
Massachusetts	x	x m[3]	x	x		
Michigan	x		x m	x m	x	x
Minnesota		x		x m		x
Mississippi		x	x d	x d		
Missouri	x		x	x	x	x
Montana			x m	x m		
Nebraska	x		x d	x m		x
Nevada		x	x m	x d		x
New Hampshire		x	x d			x
New Jersey	x		x m	x m	x	x
New Mexico	x		x p	x m		x
New York	x		x m	x m	x	
North Carolina	x		x p	x m		x
North Dakota		x		x d		
Ohio	x		xp	x m		xp

State	Income Share	Percent of Income	Extraordinary Medical Deduction	Child Care Deduction	College Support	Shared Parenting Time Offset
Oklahoma	x		xa	x m		x
Oregon	x		x p	x m	x	x
Pennsylvania	x		x m/d	x m		
Rhode Island	x		x d	x m		
South Carolina	x		x d	x m	x	
South Dakota	x		x d	x d		
Tennessee		x	x m		x[1]	x[2]
Texas		x	x m	x d		
Utah	x		x m	x m/p		x
Vermont	x		x m	x m		x
Virginia	x		x a	x a		x
Washington	x	x m[3]	x m	x		
West Virginia	x		x m	x m		x
Wisconsin		x	x m	x d		
Wyoming	x		x d	x d	x	

[1] College support may be voluntarily agreed on by the parties, in which case it is contractually enforceable, but otherwise may not be imposed by the court. However, before the child turns 18, a parent may be required to contribute to an educational trust fund that would be used for college.
[2] Support may be increased or decreased if the obligor spends more or less than 80 days than the normal amount of time with the child.
[3] Several states have elements of both the income shares and percentage of income models.

EFFECT OF JOINT CUSTODY

Questions often arise regarding the effect of joint custody on child support. The effect of joint custody will depend on the nature of the joint-custody arrangement. If the parents have **joint legal custody**—which means they share major decision making regarding the child—that fact by itself will have little effect on the issue of child support. The reason is that, even in situations of joint legal custody, one parent still has primary custody of the child and handles payment of most of the child's day-to-day expenses. The custodial parent's expenses for the child are not reduced by a joint-custody arrangement.

If the parents have **joint physical custody**, meaning that the

THE EXPENSE OF JOINT CUSTODY

In some states, the total amount that a court determines is necessary for child support may increase if the parents have joint custody and spend substantially equal time with the child. Courts or legislatures may conclude that it costs more to maintain two primary homes for the child than to maintain one primary home and another home that the child visits.

---

child spends a substantial amount of time with each parent, and if the parents have approximately equal incomes, it is possible that neither parent will have to pay support to the other. The father and mother will pay the child's day-to-day expenses when the child is in their respective homes. The parents, however, will need to coordinate payments for major expenses such as camp, school, clothing, and insurance.

If there is a significant difference in the parents' incomes, the parent with the higher income probably will make payments to the other parent or pay more of the child's expenses, but the amount paid may be less than the guideline amount because of the joint physical-custody arrangement.

CHILD SUPPORT DURING SUMMER VACATIONS

Usually, the noncustodial parent must still pay child support when the child spends summer vacations or long holiday breaks with the noncustodial parent. Courts reason that many major expenses for the benefit of the child—such as rent, mortgage, utilities, clothes, and insurance—must be paid whether the child is with the custodial parent or not. Thus, full support payments generally will remain due.

On the other hand, the court or the parties themselves are free to set payments in different amounts during vacation periods when the child is with the noncustodial parent. The lower amount of support paid during vacation periods with the noncustodial parent might reflect savings to the custodial parent for food expenses or child care.

A related issue arises if the noncustodial parent wants to reduce child support payments to the custodial parent because the noncustodial parent has spent money on the child, such as for clothes or extracurricular activities. However, such expenditures rarely constitute a legitimate basis for reducing child support payments to the custodial parent.

Court orders or divorce settlements almost always provide that child support is to be paid in specific dollar amounts from one parent to the other. Courts do not want the complication of trying to sort out whether the parties on a particular occasion agreed to an alternate way of making child support payments. Courts also do not want the noncustodial parent unilaterally changing the method of paying child support and potentially interfering with the budget planning of the custodial parent.

If the noncustodial parent wants to pay for clothes or extracurricular activities for the child, he or she is free to do. But the court will treat such payments as gifts to the child, and not as part of the noncustodial parent's support obligation.

COLLEGE EXPENSES

The obligation of a divorced parent to pay for a child's college or trade school expenses will depend on the state in which the parents live and any agreement between the parents regarding such expenses.

Courts in some states will require parents to pay for a child's college expenses, assuming the parents can afford it and the child is a good enough student to benefit from college. Courts in these states reason that the child's parents probably would have helped pay for the child's education had the marriage remained intact, and that the child's education should not suffer because of the divorce.

THE SON WHO WANTED TO GO TO DARTMOUTH

While a young man's father and mother were married, the father was very enthusiastic about his son attending Dartmouth College in New Hampshire—his alma mater. The father took his son to visit Dartmouth on three occasions, and often bought his son clothes and memorabilia bearing the Dartmouth logo. The father even arranged for influential alumni of Dartmouth to write letters of recommendation for his son. These efforts paid off, and the son was admitted to Dartmouth. At about that time, the father and mother divorced, and the father no longer wanted to pay for his son's college expenses.

In a case based on these facts, an Illinois court ruled that the father—a lawyer who earned more than $200,000 per year—was obligated to pay for his son to attend Dartmouth.

Source: In re Marriage of Campbell
(Illinois Appellate Court, 1993).

In other states, however, a parent's obligation to pay support ceases when the child reaches the age of majority or graduates high school. Thus, parents in these states are not obliged to pay for their children's college educations. Courts in these states note that married parents are not required to pay for their child's college expenses; thus, divorced parents are not required to do so either.

Regardless of a state's law regarding compulsory payment of college expenses, the mother and father can agree as part of their divorce settlement to pay for these costs. Courts usually will enforce such agreements.

Children generally are expected to help pay for their college educations and related expenses by working at summer jobs and using some of their own savings. The parents' obligation to pay, if there is such an obligation, will depend on their income and assets. A parent with low income usually will not be obligated to pay for a child's college education.

MODIFICATION OF CHILD SUPPORT

A common standard for modification of child support involves a **substantial change in circumstances**. That term usually refers to a change in income of the parent who is supposed to pay support. If that parent suffers a loss of income, courts may reduce his or her support obligation; conversely, if the parent's income increases, that obligation may increase. When a parent loses a job or experiences a financial setback, one of the last things the parent may want to do is incur more expenses by hiring an attorney to try to reduce support. But if the parent has a good reason to reduce support, that money is well spent. Unless modification is sought, the support obligation will continue at its original level; the meter on the cab will keep running at the same rate, so to speak. As an alternative to an attorney, if the local court is relatively user-friendly, the party seeking to modify his or her support obligation might try to represent himself or herself. (For more discussion of self-representation, see Chapter 15.)

Changes in the circumstances of the child can also be a reason for modifying support. If the child has significant new expenses such as orthodontia, special classes, or health needs that are not covered by insurance, that too can be a reason for increasing support.

Significant changes in the income of the parent seeking support can also be a basis for modification. If the custodial parent's income drops, particularly through no fault of his or her own, courts may be willing to increase support. Likewise, if the custodial parent's income increases, courts may reduce the support obligations of the noncustodial parent.

In some states, support orders may be reviewed automatically every few years to set support consistent with the parents' current incomes and applicable support guidelines.

If the parent who is supposed to pay support experiences a major decrease in income, for example through loss of a job, and that income is not likely to be replaced soon, the parent should promptly go to court to seek modification of child support obligations.

The obligation to pay support in the court-ordered amount continues until a court orders otherwise. However, a court's order for child support generally is effective for future support payments only. Normally, a court cannot retroactively modify support payments, even if the parent who was supposed to pay had a good reason for not making full payments.

 TALKING TO A LAWYER

Q. If my spouse and I agree between ourselves to change custody of the children, must we also modify the court order of child support, or does the support order stop automatically?

A. Court orders of child support do not stop automatically with an informal change of custody. If you want to be sure that further support is not due, or that there is an official change in the parent who is to pay support, you should have a court order that says so. Such orders can be entered by agreement, if the parties are willing. Sometimes parents will change custody on a trial basis—to see if the new arrangement works out. If the new custody or parenting-time arrangement works out and the parents are willing to continue it, they might then have the court enter an order to modify or stop support. If there was an informal change of custody that has gone on for years, and the original custodial parent—who now is no longer the child's primary caretaker—tries to collect past-due support for a period in which the child lived with the other parent, the court is less likely to require payment of support. The court would consider such payment unjustified enrichment of the parent who was not caring for the child on a day-to-day basis. Nonetheless, some courts will order payment of past-due support in such circumstances, saying that the power to set support is with the courts and not with parents.

Answer by Professor Jeff Atkinson,
DePaul University College of Law, Chicago, Illinois

Reducing Support When a Child Reaches Majority

When a child reaches the age of majority—usually eighteen—or graduates high school, child support normally stops for that child, unless the parent is obliged to help pay for that child's college education. (For a detailed discussion of college payments, see pages 155–156.)

Whether payments stop at age eighteen or upon a child's graduation from high school depends on state law. In many states, payments stop upon the later of those two events, assuming the child will graduate high school within a normal amount of time.

If only one child is the subject of a support order, the parent who is obliged to pay child support can stop making payments when the child reaches eighteen or graduates high school. The obligor does not have to go to court to seek permission to stop payments.

If there is more than one child who is the subject of a support order, the right of the obligor to reduce payments when the oldest child reaches the age of majority will depend on the wording of the court's order.

If support is set at a certain amount per child—for example, if the order indicates that "child support shall be $200 per month for each of the three children"—then the obligor may reduce payments by $200 as each of the three children reaches the age of majority. Under this example, child support would be $600 per month when all three children were under eighteen; $400 per month once the oldest child reached eighteen; $200 per month once the middle child reached eighteen; and no support would be required once all three children were over the age of eighteen.

On the other hand, if child support was ordered as a lump sum for all children—if, for example, the order indicated that "child support for the three children shall be $600 per month"—then the obligor would have to keep paying $600 per month until the youngest of the three children turned eighteen, *unless* the obligor went to court to obtain a reduction in support obligations.

Even when a child turns eighteen, the court will not reduce support automatically. Instead, it will examine a variety of factors, including the current incomes of the parents and the needs of the remaining children. If the income of the parents has remained the same and the needs of any remaining minor children are the same, an obligor could expect the support obligation for the remaining children to decrease. However, the percentage amount of reduction may vary. Thus, in the above example, the obligor's support obligation will not necessarily decrease by one-third simply because one of three children reaches majority. Applying Illinois's child support guidelines (see page 148), for example, the obligor could expect that child support payments would be reduced from 32 to 28 percent of his or her net income.

 ## TREAD CAREFULLY WHEN SEEKING TO REDUCE SUPPORT

When considering whether to go to court to seek a reduction in child support based on the oldest child reaching majority (or when seeking a reduction on some other basis), the obligor should consider how the guidelines apply to his or her *current* income. If the obligor's current income has risen significantly since the last order, a new child support order may actually require *more* support—even if there are fewer minor children—because the obligor's income has increased.

As an example, assume that at the time of his divorce five years ago, an obligor had a net income of $22,500 per year. If the obligor has three children, and Illinois guidelines applied, the obligor would pay 32 percent of his net income for child support, which is $7,200 per year, or $600 per month. Assume further that the court's order (or the parents' settlement agreement) provides that "child support for the three children shall be $600 per month." Five years later, the obligor's net income has doubled to $45,000 per year. If the obligor now wants to reduce child support because his oldest child has reached eighteen, he could be in for an unpleasant surprise.

While it is true that a child's **emancipation** (reaching the age of majority) is a basis for modifying support obligations, applying the guidelines to the obligor's *current* income would actually result in an increase in those obligations. Applying Illinois guidelines for obligors with two children, the obligor will now pay 28 percent of his net income for support. Thus, his yearly support obligation will now be $12,600—an increase of $5,400 per year over his obligations under the old order—even though he has one less child to support.

Similar considerations apply to the parent to whom support is due. If the parent receiving support has had a significant increase in income, that parent may not be able to obtain an increase in support—even if the state's guidelines or other legal principles would normally shift more of the support obligation to the parent receiving support.

The lesson? Sometimes it is best not to rush off to court, even though it may seem tempting.

UNPAID CHILD SUPPORT

Beginning in the mid-1980s, federal and state officials increased their focus on the issue of unpaid child support. Many laws were passed to improve enforcement and go after so-called deadbeats. But as with the perennial "war on crime" we hear so much about in the news, progress is slow and new laws do not provide a full solution to the problem.

The Census Bureau reports that only about half of parents entitled to receive child support receive the full amount that is due. About one-quarter of parents to whom support is due receive partial payments, and the other one-quarter receive nothing at all. In recent years, about $13 billion per year in court-ordered child support went unpaid. The federal Office of Child Support Enforcement reported that, as of 2003, the total amount of unpaid child support—referred to as **arrearage**—reached $96 billion.

In addition, there are several million mothers who have not obtained orders of child support for their children. A high percentage of these women have children who were born out of wedlock. Approximately 27 percent of custodial mothers do not have agreements or court orders that provide them with child support. By comparison, 61 percent of custodial fathers do not have orders or agreements under which the mother pays child support to the father.

For custodial parents who actually receive child support, the average amount owed is $5,044 per year, or about $420 per month. (These figures are from 2002—the last year in which a complete survey was conducted by the Census Bureau.)

Statistically, payment of child support correlates with visitation or time spent with the child. The Census Bureau reports that 77 percent of noncustodial parents with joint custody or visitation rights paid child support, whereas only 56 percent of noncustodial parents without joint custody or visitation rights paid support.

The cost of trying to collect unpaid child support is substantial. According to the U.S. Office of Child Support Enforcement, in fiscal year 2003, federal and state child support enforcement agencies spent $5.2 billion to collect about $21.2

(i) CHILD SUPPORT PAID BY FATHERS AND MOTHERS PER YEAR

	Noncustodial Fathers	Noncustodial Mothers	All Noncustodial Parents
Average support due	$5,138	$4,221	$5,044
Average support paid	$3,192	$2,881	$3,160
Percent making full payment	45.4%	39%	44.8%
Percent making any payment	74.7%	67.4%	73.9%

Source: U.S. Census Bureau (2003 report of 2002 data)

billion in child support. Each dollar of administrative costs generated about $4.13 of child support payments, although some portion of such payments would have been made even without the involvement of an enforcement agency.

ENFORCEMENT

State and federal governments use a variety of techniques to enforce payment of child support.

Wage Deduction Orders

The most common enforcement tool is a **wage deduction order,** in which a court orders an employer to send a portion of the obligor-parent's wages to a state agency, which then sends the money to the custodial parent.

Beginning in 1994, all new child support orders were required to provide for an automatic deduction from the obligor's wages. The wage deduction takes effect immediately unless the parties have agreed otherwise, or unless a court waives immediate deductions from wages—and even then, the order must provide that a wage deduction will begin automatically if the person owing child support falls more than thirty days behind in payments. Wage withholding can be used to collect current support as well as past-due support.

Wage deduction orders are effective in collecting support if a parent is regularly employed and does not change jobs frequently. However, if the parent loses a job, there is no wage from which to make a deduction. And if the parent changes jobs, the new employer must be served with a deduction notice before wages can be withheld.

If a parent is self-employed, he or she is still obliged to make payments, but the person to whom support is due cannot look to an independent employer to make sure that the payments are sent on time.

Tax Refunds

For parents who are behind in support payments, the state also can intercept federal and state tax refunds. This is a useful remedy if the obligor-parent has a sizeable refund due. If the obligor filed a joint income tax return with a new spouse, the new spouse can show the enforcement authorities the portion of the income tax refund that belongs to him or her and prevent that portion of the refund from being intercepted. In addition to seizing tax refunds, states also can place liens on property, such as real estate and automobiles, to obtain past-due support.

License Revocation

In another technique for enforcing payment of child support, the granting or renewal of certain types of licenses is made contingent on the payment of support. If an obligor does not pay support, the obligor could lose his or her driver's license or professional license—such as a license to practice law or medicine or work as a barber, beautician, or plumber.

Maine was one of the first states to enact legislation making licenses—including driver's licenses, business licenses, and even fishing licenses—contingent upon payment of child support. Maine reported that as of 1999, it collected approximately $116 million in past-due support as a result of the program. Maine found that the threat of license revocation often was enough to induce prompt payment. Of 23,500 persons who received warning letters from the state, more than half of those persons made payments or entered into written agreements to make payments.

Proponents of this technique appreciate the comparative simplicity of the approach. License revocation, or threats of revocation, can be handled administratively. In some states such as Maine, court hearings are not necessary as they are with some other remedies, such as actions for contempt of court.

Opponents of such programs are concerned that the system may not adequately take into account the hardship to an obligor who has lost a job or income and cannot afford to pay. If an

TAX INTERCEPTS

As a practical matter, tax interception as a means of enforcing support payments usually is helpful for a period of only one year. The reason is that, once an obligor-parent has had a substantial tax refund seized, that parent often adjusts deductions of taxes from wages so that refunds in future years will be minimal.

obligor's driver's license or professional license is revoked, the obligor's ability to pay may be harmed further.

Contempt of Court

Another penalty that states may impose on parents who have not paid support is to find such parents in **contempt of court**. A finding of contempt means that the person charged has willfully failed to do something ordered by the court—in this case, pay child support. A finding of contempt can result in a fine, a jail term, or both. If the parent cannot pay support for a good reason, such as loss of a job by no fault of his or her own, a court will not find the parent in contempt, but the obligation to pay support will continue.

THE UNIFORM INTERSTATE FAMILY SUPPORT ACT

To enforce child support orders when a child lives in one state and the obligor lives in another state, laws can be used to establish support orders and collect payments. The main law in this area is the Uniform Interstate Family Support Act (UIFSA). All fifty states have adopted UIFSA, or different versions of it. A key provision of the act provides for "**continuing, exclusive jurisdiction**" of states over obligors. This means that once a state enters a valid child support order, no other state may modify that order as long as either of the parties—or the child for whose benefit the order was entered—continue to live in that state. Thus, if a parent wants to modify a child support order, the parent needs to do it in the state where the order was entered.

If all parties and the child have left the state and one party wishes to modify the order, that party must submit himself or herself to the jurisdiction where the other party resides. For example, assume a mother and father obtain a divorce in Minnesota, where they lived during most of their marriage. After the divorce, the mother and child move to Wisconsin, and the father moves to Iowa. If the mother seeks to increase child support, she would need to have the case decided by the Iowa courts where the father lives. If the father seeks to reduce child support, he would need to have the case decided by the Wisconsin courts where the mother lives.

ASSISTANCE IN ENFORCING CHILD SUPPORT ORDERS

If you need assistance in seeking to enforce an order for past-due child support, you have several options.

State and District Attorneys

State attorneys and district attorneys are available to help with collection of child support, though their efficiency varies from district to district. Some parents to whom support is due have complained of delays in such attorneys' handling of support claims. State attorneys provide their services at no cost to parents who are receiving public aid. If parents do not receive public aid, a state attorney can still provide assistance, but a small charge—usually less than $25—may apply.

Private Attorneys

Private attorneys can also help parents with collection of child support. The attorney's normal rates will usually apply, though some attorneys may be willing the handle the case for a **contingency fee**. This means the lawyer will take a portion of whatever is collected, but the client will not have to pay the attorney if nothing is collected. The permissibility of using contingency fees to collect past-due support varies from state to state. The amount of such fees also varies, but a payment to the attorney of one-third of the amount collected is a common arrangement.

Attorney's fees also can be assessed against the party who failed to pay support, in which case that party will pay for the attorney of the other parent in addition to his or her own attorney's fees.

Collection Agencies

Another way of collecting past-due child support is to use a collection agency. Some collection agencies will handle collection of child support just as they handle collection of business debts or credit card debts. Collection agencies usually charge a contingency fee. Such agencies can be found using the yellow pages—particularly the volume devoted to business-related services, if there is one.

Federal Prosecution

Although prosecutors involved in punishing parents who do not pay child support usually work for state or county governments, federal prosecutors can get involved too. In 1992, Congress passed the **Child Support Recovery Act**, which makes it a federal crime to willfully fail to pay child support to a child who resides in another state if the past-due amount has been unpaid for more than one year or exceeds $5,000. Punishments under the federal law include up to six months imprisonment and a $5,000 fine for a first offense, and up to two years imprisonment and a $250,000 fine for a repeat offense.

Federal prosecutors are not the primary enforcers of past-due child support payments. Most U.S. attorneys prefer to use their resources for larger-scale criminal activity, although they may pursue some of the more egregious cases of past-due support. For parents seeking government help in collecting child support, local prosecutors are likely to have more to offer than federal prosecutors, unless the amount of past-due support is very large and the obligor lives in a different state than the parent to whom support is due.

One egregious case that arose before passage of the federal law was handled by Arizona prosecutors. A thirty-five-year-old man was ordered to pay $600 per month in support for his three children, but according to Arizona child support officials, he never made a single payment. The man moved from state to state, changing the spelling of his name and his Social Security number four times in an effort to avoid collection attempts. When prosecutors finally caught up with him ten years after the original support order, the man owed $108,000 in past-due support and interest. He was sentenced to one and one-half years in prison.

Most parents who owe support do not make a career out of avoiding their support obligations. Nonetheless, enforcement of support often can be difficult.

 COLLECTING PAST-DUE CHILD SUPPORT

The following is a list of techniques for collecting past-due child support:

Wage withholding orders. Wage withholding orders are entered by a court and served on the employer of the parent who owes support. The employer sends payments to the government, which then sends support payments to the parent to whom support is owed.

Refund intercepts. The government sends a notice to the Internal Revenue Service or the state department of revenue directing that the obligor's tax refund be sent to the government for payment of support.

Liens on property. A lien can be placed on the real estate, automobile, or other property of the obligor. If support is not paid, the property can be confiscated and sold. Alternatively, the lien may stay on the property until it is sold by the obligor, at which point the debt must be paid before the obligor receives any proceeds from the sale.

Contempt of court. The government or the person to whom support is due can ask a court to hold the obligor in contempt of court for willful failure to pay support. If found guilty of contempt, the obligor can be jailed, fined, or both.

Collection agencies. Some collection agencies are willing to help collect past-due support, just as they collect past-due commercial debts. Collection agencies usually charge a portion of the amount collected.

Revocation of licenses. Many states will revoke the driver's license or professional licenses of persons who have not paid child support.

Establishing a trust. If it appears likely that an obligor will not make future child support payments, but the obligor has assets from which support could be paid, in some states a court can order the obligor to establish a trust for the benefit of the child, thus ensuring that funds are available to pay support.

CHILD SUPPORT AND VISITATION

Child support and visitation are independent rights and obligations. If a parent is not receiving child support, the remedy for that parent is to go to court—or activate a wage withholding order—to collect child support. The parent who is supposed to receive child support may not deny visitation or contact with the child because support has not been paid.

Similarly, if visitation or contact with the child is blocked by the custodial parent, the legal remedy for the noncustodial parent is to go to court to obtain an order enforcing visitation. The noncustodial parent may not cut off or reduce child support because the custodial parent interfered with visitation.

THE WORLD AT YOUR FINGERTIPS

• For detailed information on child support, including links to each state's child support guidelines, visit the Child Support Guidelines website at *www.childsupportguidelines.com.*

• For online calculators to determine child support under each state's laws, visit AllLaw.com: *www.alllaw.com/calculators/ChildSupport.*

• For hardbooks and factsheets about child suppport enforcement, visit the website of the federal government's Office of Child Support Enforcement at *www.acf.hhs.gov/programs/cse.*

REMEMBER THIS

• The legislatures or courts of each state have adopted guidelines to establish child support. These guidelines are based on the number of children who require support and the income of the noncustodial parent or both parents. Additional factors considered in setting child support include: child care expenses, the cost of health insurance, special needs of the child, and other financial obligations of the parents.

• Many techniques are used to enforce payment of child support, including wage deductions, interception of tax refunds, liens on property, revocation of drivers' licenses and professional licenses, findings of contempt of court (which can entail fines and jail time), and criminal prosecution.

CHAPTER 13
Custody and Parenting Time

Susan and Jim have been married for twelve years, and have two children: a boy, age ten, and a girl, age eight. Both parents have been involved in the day-to-day raising of their children. Susan has served as a room parent at the children's school. Jim coaches the children's soccer teams. When filing for divorce, each parent sought primary custody. Susan and Jim are of different religions and want to raise the children in their respective faiths. The children do not have strong preferences about custody arrangements; they wish their parents would get back together. How will a court decide custody?

Child custody is the right to care, custody, and control of a child on a day-to-day basis, and the right to make major decisions about the child.

In **sole custody** arrangements, one parent takes care of the child most of the time and makes major decisions about the child. That parent usually is called the **custodial parent**. The other parent generally is referred to as the **noncustodial parent**. The noncustodial parent almost always has a right to **parenting time**, or **visitation**—a right to be with the child, including for overnight visits and vacation periods.

In **joint custody** arrangements, both parents share in making major decisions, and both parents also might spend substantial amounts of time with the child.

As is the case with financial issues in a divorce, most divorcing spouses reach an agreement about custody before they go to court. Fewer than 5 percent of parents have child custody issues decided by a judge.

When parents cannot agree as to custody of their child, the court decides custody issues based on what it deems the **best interest of the child**. Determining the best interest of the child involves consideration of many factors. These factors often are listed in states' family law statutes, domestic-relations statutes, and court decisions. (These factors, along with more information about visitation and joint custody, will be discussed later in this chapter.)

EVOLUTION OF CUSTODY STANDARDS

The law of child custody has swung like a pendulum. From the early history of our country until the mid-1800s, fathers were favored for custody in the event of divorce. If a husband and wife divorced, the man usually received the property—such as the farm or the family business. Since children were viewed as similar to property, he also received custody of the children. Some courts viewed giving custody to the father as a natural extension of the father's duty to support and educate his children.

By the mid-1800s, most states had come to exhibit a strong preference for the mother in issues of custody. This preference was based on assumptions often referred to as the **tender-years doctrine** or **maternal presumption**. Under the tender-years doctrine, the mother received custody as long as she was minimally fit. In other words, in a contested custody case, a mother would receive custody unless she was patently unfit—as in the case of mental illness, alcoholism, or an abusive relationship with her child. The parenting skills of the father were not relevant.

The automatic preference for mothers continued until the 1960s or 1980s, depending on the state, when principles of equality mandated that the custody decision be gender neutral.

PREFERENCES FOR MOTHERS
OR FATHERS

Under the current law of almost all states, mothers and fathers have an equal right to custody. Courts are not supposed to assume that a child is automatically better off with the mother or the father. In a contested custody case, both parents have an equal burden of proving to the court that the best interest of the child are served by awarding them custody.

A few states—mostly in the South—have laws providing that, all other factors being equal, courts may display a preference for the mother in issues of custody. But even in those states, many fathers have been successful in obtaining custody, even in cases where the mother is a fit parent.

In some states, courts give equal consideration to mothers and fathers in deciding custody, but nonetheless deem it permissible to consider a child's age or sex when deciding custody. This usually translates to a preference for mothers in cases where the children are young or female. Again, however, it is possible for fathers in these states to gain custody, even in cases where the mother is a fit parent.

Although judges are trained to be neutral in custody disputes between mothers and fathers, some people may feel that a judge is biased toward parents of a particular gender. An advantage of having an attorney experienced in family law cases is that the attorney may know which judges have a reputation for favoring one gender over another. The attorney also may know what types of evidence will appeal to the judge and which types will not.

In many jurisdictions, it is possible to obtain a change of judge simply by asking. In some states, a litigant is entitled to one change of judge without having to present a reason for the change. The request, however, must be made before the judge has ruled on substantive issues in the case.

If a case is transferred to a judge whom you or your attorneys dislike, it will be difficult to obtain a second change. Because they do not wish to allow parties to keep shopping for judges, courts are usually unwilling to order a second change unless there is a clear, specific showing of prejudice by the judge to whom the case has been transferred. If you are before a judge whom you believe to be biased, and a change cannot be obtained, sometimes you must simply present the strongest case possible and hope for the best.

Possible Prejudice in Favor of Mothers

Judges, based on their backgrounds or personal experiences, may have a deep-seated belief that mothers can take care of children better than fathers, and that fathers have little experience in parenting. Such judges may carry those views onto the bench, in which case a father may have a very difficult time gaining primary custody.

A Louisiana case illustrates this point. In that case, the trial judge awarded custody to the mother, saying "[i]t is just a physiological fact that girl children should be with their mother[s]." Since the trial judge's bias was clear on the record, the appellate court reversed the decision and ordered further proceedings that did not apply improper presumptions based on the sex of the parents. In cases in which the trial judge is less explicit about his or her prejudice, however, it may be more difficult to obtain a reversal.

Possible Prejudice in Favor of Fathers

As noted in the previous section's discussion of the evolution of custody standards, prejudice based on the sex of parents is not a one-way street. Sometimes prejudice runs in favor of fathers.

Some judges tend automatically to favor fathers, particularly if the children in question are boys. In an Iowa case, for example, a trial judge awarded custody of two boys, ages nine and eleven, to their father, arguing that the father would "be able to engage in various activities with [the] boys, such as athletic events, fishing, hunting, mechanical training and other activities boys are interested in."

The trouble was that the evidence before the court did not support the judge's presumption. The record in the case did not show that the boys were interested in hunting or mechanical training or that the father's skills in those areas were superior to the mother's. In fact, the mother went fishing with the boys more often than did the father.

The Iowa Supreme Court reversed the trial court's decision and awarded custody to the mother, who had been primarily responsible for raising the children. The court stated that "[t]he real issue is not the sex of the parent but which parent will do better in raising the children. It logically follows that neither parent has an edge based on the sex of the children either."

Another possible prejudice in favor of fathers may arise as the result of prejudice against working mothers. In some cases, it appears that judges have looked askance at working mothers, perhaps holding mothers to a higher standard than fathers and assuming that working mothers do not serve the best interests of their children. Such judges also may view as exceptional a father who shows slightly-above-average involvement in parenting and thus reward him with custody particularly where the father has remarried and his new wife can also care for the child.

It is difficult to assess how widespread this view may be among judges. Some commentators assert that bias against working mothers, especially professional women, may be a significant factor. Others suggest that a review of appellate court cases does not disclose widespread prejudice against working mothers, although such prejudice does exist to some degree. If anything, most judges seem to admire a mother (or father) who can simultaneously manage work and raising children.

A parent's work schedule normally is not a decisive factor in custody cases, unless there is a major difference in the amount

 SINGLE PARENTS

The U.S. Census Bureau reports that in 2003 there were 12.4 million households headed by single parents living with their own children under the age of eighteen. Of those households, 10.1 million (81 percent) were headed by mothers and 2.3 million (19 percent) were headed by fathers.

of time each parent can spend with the child. If after a divorce, one parent will be able to spend much more time with the child than the other parent, that fact may weigh in favor of the parent with the more flexible schedule.

FACTORS CONSIDERED IN DETERMINING CUSTODY

There is no one factor that is determinative in every custody case. If one parent in a custody dispute has a major problem—such as alcoholism, mental illness, or an abusive relationship with the child—that problem of course will weigh heavily against that parent in a custody decision. Otherwise, the importance of various factors will depend on the facts of each case.

Primary Caretaker of the Child

If neither parent has engaged in unusually bad conduct, a custody decision may largely depend on which parent has been primarily responsible for the care of child on a day-to-day basis. Some states refer to this as the **primary-caretaker factor**. If one parent can show that he or she took care of the child most of the time, that parent usually will be favored for custody, particularly if the child is young—that is, under about eight years of age.

Application of the primary-caretaker factor promotes continuity in the child's life and awards custody of the child to the more experienced parent—the parent who is more familiar with the child's day-to-day needs. If both parents have actively cared for the child or if the child is older, this factor is less crucial, though it may still be considered.

Preferences of the Child

The wishes of a child can be an important factor in deciding custody. The weight a court gives to a child's wishes will depend on the child's age and maturity, and the quality of his or her reasons. Some judges will not even listen to the preferences of a child under the age of seven, and instead assume such children are too young to express informed preferences.

A court is more likely to consider the preferences of an older child, though the court will want to assess the quality of the child's reasons. If a child wants to be with the parent who offers more freedom and less discipline, a judge is not likely to honor the preference. A child whose reasons are vague or whose answers seem coached also may not have his or her preferences honored.

On the other hand, if a child expresses a good reason related to his or her best interest, such as genuinely feeling closer to one parent than the other, the court probably will honor his or her preference. Although most states treat a child's wishes as only one factor to be considered, one state—Georgia—declares that a child of fourteen has an "absolute right" to choose the parent with whom he or she will live, as long as the parent is fit.

If a judge decides to talk with a child, he or she usually will do so in private—in chambers rather than in open court. Generally, the parents are not in the room when a judge talks to a child, although the parents' attorneys might be. In some cases, the judge

 TOO MANY GIFTS TO THE CHILD

In one Louisiana case, a thirteen-year-old boy who was living with his mother said that he wanted to live with his father. In the weeks before the court hearing to modify custody, the father had presented his son with a series of gifts based on the song *The Twelve Days of Christmas*. The gifts included: one horse, two color television sets, a shotgun, a minibike, a motorcycle, and a private telephone. The court ruled that the boy would stay with his mother.

Source: Johnson v. McCullough (*Louisiana Supreme Court 1982*).

may appoint a mental-health professional, such as a psychiatrist, psychologist, or social worker, to talk to the child and report to the court. In addition, a court may appoint an **attorney for the child,** or **guardian ad litem** (**GAL**), to present the child's views and other relevant information to the court.

Nonmarital Sexual Relationships

The impact of a parent's nonmarital sexual relationships on a custody determination depends on state law and on the facts of the case. In most states, affairs or nonmarital sexual relationships are not a factor in deciding custody, unless it can be shown that such relationships have harmed the child or are likely to harm the child in the future.

For example, one parent having a discreet affair during his or her marriage normally would not factor significantly into a court's custody decision. Similarly, if a parent lives with a person to whom he or she is not married after the end of his or her marriage, the live-in relationship by itself will not normally have a significant effect on a court's custody decision. In the case of live-in relationships, however, the quality of the relationship between the child and the live-in partner can be an important factor in a custody dispute.

If the parent's nonmarital sexual relationship or relationships have placed the child in embarrassing situations or caused significant stress to the child, then those relationships might factor negatively against the parent involved in them. In one case, for example, a mother conducted an affair during her marriage with a man who lived in the neighborhood. She and the neighbor met periodically in the woman's bedroom while her husband was out and her child was at home. This placed the child in a stressful situation—a situation that grew worse when the neighbor's wife appeared at the door and demanded that the child reveal what his mother and the neighbor were doing in the bedroom. In that case, the mother lost custody primarily because of her nonmarital relationship and its impact on her child.

CYBERSEX

A mother and father disputed custody of their three-year-old son. When the child was two years old, the mother admitted that she engaged in "highly erotic" discourse in Internet chat rooms with two different adult men. These communications occurred, according to her estimate, perhaps once a week. She explained to the court that "it was kind of enjoyable that someone was finding interest in me."

The trial court found that the mother's conduct was "potentially harmful" and "appalling," but that there was no "demonstrable effect" on the child. The trial court also found that both parents were good caregivers, and that the mother had been the primary caregiver of the child. The trial court granted custody to the mother, and the South Dakota Supreme Court upheld the decision.

Source: Zepeda v. Zepeda (*South Dakota Supreme Court, 2001*).

Although most states require a specific showing of harm to the child before nonmarital sexual conduct will be factored into a custody decision, courts in a few states are more inclined to assume automatically that such conduct is or will be harmful to the child. As with the issue of gender-based parental preferences, the issue of a parent's sexual conduct can be one in which individual judges may have personal feelings that influence their decisions.

Homosexual Relationships

The impact of a parent's homosexual relationships on custody decisions varies significantly from state to state. Courts in some states may assume that a parent's homosexual relationship will

IMPORTANT EVIDENCE

Whether heterosexual or homosexual, a parent who is in a relationship and seeking custody will have a stronger case if he or she presents evidence that the child has not witnessed sexual contact between the partners, and that the child likes the parent's partner.

have a more harmful impact on a child than a heterosexual relationship. On the other hand, some states treat homosexual and heterosexual relationships equally and will not consider homosexual relationships to be a significant factor in custody decisions unless specific harm to the child is shown.

Undermining of the Child's Relationship with the Other Parent

Most states have a specific policy favoring an ongoing, healthy relationship between the child and both parents. If one parent tries to undermine the child's relationship with the other parent, that attempt may factor against him or her in a court's custody decision. All other factors being roughly equal, a court may grant custody to the parent who is more likely to encourage an open and positive relationship with the other parent.

Similarly, if a custodial parent regularly interferes with visitation, that may factor against him or her in a custody decision, and could trigger a transfer of custody to the noncustodial parent—assuming the noncustodial parent is able to care for the child properly.

Religious Beliefs and Practices

Under the First Amendment to the U.S. Constitution, both parents have a right to practice religion or not practice religion as

THE FIRST AMENDMENT TO THE U.S. CONSTITUTION

The First Amendment to the U.S. Constitution reads: "Congress shall make no law respecting an establishment of religion, or prohibiting the free exercise thereof; or abridging the freedom of speech, or of the press; or the right of the people peaceably to assemble, and to petition the government for a redress of grievances."

they see fit. A judge is not supposed to make value judgments about whether a child is better off with or without religious training or about which religion is better. If a child has been brought up with particular religious beliefs and religious activities are important to the child, a court might favor promoting continuity in the child's life, but the court should not favor religion per se.

In some cases, a parent's unusual or nonmainstream religious activities may become an issue. Normally, a court should not consider a parent's unusual religious practices in deciding custody or visitation unless specific harm to the child is shown. If, because of a parent's religious beliefs, a parent has not given the child needed medical care or has tried to negatively influence the child's opinion of the other parent, that behavior could constitute grounds for awarding custody to the parent whose religious conduct does not harm the child.

MODIFICATION OF CUSTODY

Courts have the power to modify child custody arrangements to meet the needs of the child and to respond to changes in the parents' lives. A parent seeking to modify custody through the court usually must show that circumstances have changed substantially since the last custody order. Changes warranting such

TWO CASES ABOUT RELIGION

In a California case, a mother sought to obtain a restraining order prohibiting the father from engaging in any religious activities or discussions with their six- and seven-year-old children during his visitation. The father was a member of The Church of Jesus Christ of Latter-day Saints (the Mormon Church). The mother was a member of the Los Gatos Christian Church. The mother and a court conciliator testified that the children were confused about doctrinal differences between the father's church and the mother's church. The mother admitted that her church was hostile to the Mormon Church. The California Court of Appeals ruled that the mother's claims of harm were "manifestly insufficient" and "essentially conjectural," and that an order prohibiting the father from engaging in religious activities with his children "represents an unwarranted intrusion into family privacy."

Source: **In re Marriage of Mentry** (*California Appellate Court, 1983*).

In a Vermont case, a mother sought to modify a joint parenting agreement to grant her sole custody, and to obtain an order preventing the father from bringing their children to Jehovah's Witness gatherings. The mother, the children's pediatrician, and the children's counselor presented "extensive evidence" that the parties' daughters were experiencing "extreme confusion and anxiety," including nightmares, stomachaches, and thumb sucking. In addition, numerous conflicts arose from the children's exposure to the religion, including disagreements over whether the children should participate in birthday and holiday celebrations at school. The Vermont Supreme Court affirmed the trial court's ruling granting sole custody to the mother, and ordered that the father not bring the children to Jehovah's Witness gatherings. The court noted the harm to the children that had arisen from the parents' conflicting religious views and from the father's attempt to alienate the children from their mother. Moreover, the supreme court noted that the trial court had not been "in the position of picking a religion for the children, but was only giving effect to the mother's decision on that issue [regarding the children's religious upbringing]."

Source: Meyer v. Meyer (*Vermont Supreme Court, 2001*).

modification usually involve something negative in the child's current environment—such as improper supervision, or harmful conflicts with the custodial parent or stepparent.

In addition to showing a change in circumstances, the parent seeking a change of custody must show that he or she can provide a better environment for the child than the child's current environment.

A child's preference to live with the noncustodial parent can be a basis for modifying custody, but the child's reasons must be well-based and not appear to be the result of coaching or bribery.

In order to discourage parents from constantly litigating custody, some states apply a special standard for custody modifications sought within the first year or two after a prior custody order. In those states, the parent must show not only a change of circumstances, but also that the child is endangered by his or her current environment. After expiration of the one- or two-year period, the courts apply normal standards for modification, without requiring parents to show endangerment.

If parents voluntarily wish to change custody or a child's visitation schedule (see below), they may do so without having to prove special factors such as endangerment or a change in circumstances. Parents may change custody and visitation without obtaining a court order, but if the parent receiving custody or more visitation wants to make the modification "official"—thus making it more difficult for the other parent to revert to the old system—it is best to obtain a court order to that effect.

In addition, an informal change of custody will not necessarily terminate a parent's support obligation—only a new court order can change court-ordered child support.

TALKING TO A LAWYER

Q. Can courts take race into account when they are making custody decisions?

A. The U.S. Supreme Court has ruled that a parent's race is not a permissible factor in deciding a custody dispute between a mother and father. In the 1984 case of *Palmore v. Sidotti*, a mother and father, both white, were divorced, and the mother and father agreed that the mother would have custody of their three-year-old daughter. Sixteen months later, the father filed a petition to change custody based on changed circumstances. The change of circumstances was the mother's cohabitation with a black man, whom she married two months later.

The trial court found that there was no issue regarding the quality of the home either parent could offer to the child, and no issue regarding the respectability of either parent's new spouse. The trial court said that the father's resentment of the mother's black partner was not sufficient reason for taking custody from the mother. But the court added that when the girl attained school age and was subject to peer pressure, "it is inevitable that [the girl] will . . . suffer from the social stigmatization that is sure to come." On that basis, the trial court awarded custody to the father. The Florida appellate court affirmed the trial court's decision.

The U.S. Supreme Court reversed the earlier decisions based on the equal protection clause of the Fourteenth Amendment. The Court held that classifications based on race are "subject to the most exacting scrutiny; to pass constitutional muster, they must be justified by a compelling governmental interest and must be 'necessary . . . to the accomplishment' of its legitimate purpose." The Court acknowledged that a child living with a stepparent of a different race may be subject to prejudice. The Court went on to say, however, that "[t]he Constitution cannot control such prejudices but neither can it tolerate them. Private biases may be outside the reach of the law, but the law cannot, directly or indirectly, give them effect." The custody decision, which was based on the race of the child's stepparent, was reversed.

Answer by Professor Jeff Atkinson,
DePaul University College of Law, Chicago, Illinois

VISITATION

A parent who does not receive custody normally is entitled to **parenting time**—or **visitation**—with the child. The amount of visitation will vary with the desires of the parents and the inclinations of the judge. However, a common visitation arrangement includes: every other weekend (Friday evening through Sunday); a weeknight (for dinner); half of the child's winter and spring breaks, alternate major holidays; Father's Day or Mother's Day, as applicable; and two to six weeks in the summer.

If parents live far apart and regular weekend visitation is not feasible, it is common to allocate more summer vacation and school holidays to the noncustodial parent.

For parents who do not like the terms "visitation" or "custody," it is possible to draft custody and visitation orders that eliminate those terms entirely and simply describe the times during which the child will be with each parent. In addition, since the mid-1990s, the term "parenting time" has increasingly replaced the term "visitation."

A court can deny or restrict visitation if it believes the child might be endangered by such visitation. For example, if the non-custodial parent has molested the child, is likely to kidnap the child, or is likely to use illegal drugs or excessive amounts of alcohol while caring for the child, a court will probably deny or restrict visitation. If visitation is restricted, it might be allowed only with supervision, such as at a social-service agency or in the company of a responsible relative.

VERY SPECIFIC CUSTODY AND VISITATION ORDERS

If parents are prone to conflict or if they prefer a high level of detail, they may wish to create very specific custody and visitation orders addressing a multitude of issues. Such orders might include the following details:

- Specification of weekends for visitation. For maximum clarity, the parties might specify the precise weekends during which visitation will occur—for example, "weekends beginning on the first, third, and fifth Fridays of the month," as opposed to simply "every other weekend."

- Lists of holidays, winter breaks, and spring breaks. For maximum clarity, the agreement might specify that certain holiday visitations will take place during odd- or even-numbered years—as opposed to simply "every other year."

- Allocation of special school holidays and institute days, which may not be the same as legal holidays.

- Specific pick-up and drop-off times.

- Specification of which parent will hold birthday parties to which the child invites friends. (The parties may wish to assume this role in alternate years.)

- Periods of notice required for choosing summer vacation time with the children.

- Requirements for notification of the child's whereabouts when he or she will be out of town.

- Agreement for the parents to reasonably accommodate each other in situations where one parent must travel out of town on business, or where that parent is otherwise unable to be with the children for a designated period of time.

- Agreement for the parents to share or provide copies of school and medical records (federal law requires that both parents have access to school records unless a court orders otherwise).

- Agreement for each parent to notify the other of teacher conferences, athletic events, and other events involving the child.

- Agreement for the parents to consult with each other about extracurricular activities in which the child will be involved.

- Agreement to make the child available for special events regardless of the custody or visitation schedule—for example, to make the child available for family weddings, reunions, and funerals.

- Agreement for each parent to allow the child telephone or Internet contact with the other parent. For maximum clarity, the parties may wish to specify allowable times and frequency of such contact.

- Agreement to encourage, or at least not interfere with, the child's relationship with the other parent.

- Agreement to notify the other parent of any change in address, telephone number, or employment.

JOINT CUSTODY

Joint custody—sometimes referred to as **shared custody** or **shared parenting**—has two components: joint legal custody and joint physical custody. A joint custody order can address one or both of these components.

With **joint legal custody,** both parents share in major decisions affecting the child. A custody order may describe the issues about which the parents must share decisions. The most common of these issues are school, health care, and religious training— although, as discussed earlier, both parents have a right to expose the child to their respective religious beliefs. Other issues about which parents may make joint decisions include: extracurricular activities, summer camp, the appropriate age for dating or driving, and methods of discipline.

Many joint custody orders specify procedures parents should follow in the event they cannot agree on an issue. The most common procedure is for the parents to consult a mediator. (Mediation will be discussed in Chapter 16.)

With **joint physical custody,** a child spends time with each of his or her parents. The amount of time spent with each parent is flexible. It may be relatively moderate—for example, the child could spend every other weekend with one parent—or the child's time could be equally divided between the parents. Parents who opt for equal time-sharing have come up with many possible arrangements, such as: alternate weeks, alternate two-day periods; equal division of each week; alternate months; and alternate six-month periods.

If the child is attending school and spends a substantial amount of time with both parents, it usually is best for the child if the parents live relatively close to each other. Some parents, on an interim basis, have kept the child in a single home while the parents rotate, each staying in the home with the child during specified times.

In most states, joint custody is an option, just as sole custody is an option. Courts may order joint custody or sole custody based on what the judge believes to be in the best interest of the child. In some states—eleven states and the District of Columbia in 2003—legislatures have declared a general preference for joint custody. This means that the courts are supposed to order joint custody if one parent asks for it, unless there is a good reason for not doing so. In twelve other states, there is a presumption in favor of joint custody if both parents ask for it.

The most common reason for not ordering joint custody is the parents' inability to cooperate. Courts are concerned that a

 REVIEWING PARENTING PLANS

Children's needs with respect to each parent change as the children grow older. As a result, parents probably should avoid committing permanently to any one parenting plan. Rather, the parents should plan to review custody and parenting arrangements as their children grow and their needs change.

child will be caught in the middle of a tug-of-war if joint custody is ordered for parents who do not cooperate. Parents who do not cooperate also will have trouble with sole custody and visitation arrangements, but the frequency of conflicts may be somewhat reduced, since they will need to confer less often on major decisions and the logistics of physical custody.

Supporters of joint physical custody stress that it is in the

 CUSTODY OF BARNEY THE DOG

The attachment of humans to their pets can be profound. In a Pennsylvania case, a man sought an injunction to mandate "shared custody" of Barney, a dog purchased by his wife from an animal shelter during their marriage. The written agreement between the parties provided that "Barney is [the wife's] property and she will have full custody." The agreement also provided that the husband would be able to visit Barney. When the wife moved to a new county, however, she no longer made the dog available for visitation.

The trial court dismissed the husband's request for shared custody and the Superior Court affirmed, stating:

> In seeking "shared custody" and a "visitation" arrangement, Appellant appears to treat Barney, a dog, as a child. Despite the status owners bestow on their pets, Pennsylvania law considers dogs to be personal property. . . . The Agreement in question explicitly awarded this property to Appellee. . . . Appellant, however, overlooks the fact that any terms set forth in the Agreement are void to the extent that they attempt to award custodial visitation with or shared custody of personal property. . . . As the trial court aptly noted, Appellant is seeking an arrangement analogous, in law, to a visitation schedule for a table or a lamp. This result is clearly not contemplated by the statute.

Source: **Desanctis v. Pritchard** (*Pennsylvania Superior Court, 2002*).

best interest of the child to protect and improve the child's relationship with both parents. They believe that shared custody is the best way to ensure that a child does not "lose" a parent as a result of divorce. Supporters of joint custody also argue that it is the natural right of parents to be joint custodians of their children, whether the parents are married or not.

Critics of joint custody fear that joint custody is often unworkable, and worry about instability and potential conflict for the child. The success of joint physical custody may depend on the child. Some researchers have said that children who are relatively relaxed and laid-back will fare better in joint physical custody arrangements than children who are tense and easily upset by changes in routine. Because joint physical custody usually requires two homes for the child, joint physical custody often costs more than sole custody.

OUT-OF-STATE MOVES WITH THE CHILD

The right of a parent to move out of state with a child is another area of law on which states are divided. In times past, most states would automatically allow a custodial parent to move wherever he or she wanted with a child.

In recent years, however, some states have placed restrictions on the right of a custodial parent to move with a child. These states have a strong policy in favor of preserving continuity in the relationship between the child and noncustodial parent, and courts in these states are reluctant to allow the custodial parent to move with the child over the objection of the noncustodial parent unless there is a very good reason for the move.

In these states, the law may say a child cannot be moved without permission of the other parent or permission of the court. A parent who seeks to move with the child may be required to give notice—often sixty days notice—before a proposed moving date.

The law in this area is shifting. Some state legislatures and courts are considering new standards for determining when a parent can move out of state with a child. Regardless of the law in a particular state, however, there are several factors that courts will consider when deciding whether to allow such a move:

- **The custodial parent's reason for the move.** If the parent who seeks to move with the child has a good-faith reason for the move, a court is more likely to approve it. Good-faith reasons include: obtaining a better job, joining a new spouse, and moving to be near extended family. If a job change is the basis for the move, the plan for a new job should be specific—as opposed to a general desire to find new employment. The most common bad-faith reason for moving is to deprive the noncustodial parent of contact with a child. If the court believes this to be the custodial parent's primary motivation, it is not likely to allow the move.

- **The noncustodial parent's reason for opposing the move.** If the noncustodial parent has a good reason for opposing the move, the court will be more likely to deny permission for the move. The strongest reason for opposing relocation is the existence of a close relationship between the child and the noncustodial parent, and concern over the disruption of frequent contact between the child and the noncustodial parent. If the noncustodial parent is not close to the child or has not regularly exercised visitation, the court is more likely to allow the move.

- **Advantages to the child that may result from the move.** If it can be shown that the child will benefit from the move, a court will be more likely to approve. If, for example, the child will attend a better school or live in a climate that is better for his or her health, the court will be more likely to favor the move. The parent who asserts that the child will benefit from relocation should be ready with specific evidence, such as witnesses knowledgeable about the difference in school systems or medical testimony regarding the child's health. Some courts will assume that if the custodial parent will benefit from the move, such as through happiness at a new job or with a new spouse, the child also will benefit. Other courts do not make such an assumption, and require more specific proof of some benefit to the child.

- **The degree to which visitation can be restructured to preserve the relationship between the child and the noncustodial parent.** If the court believes that reasonable restructuring of visitation can preserve and promote a good relationship between the child and the noncustodial parent, it is more likely to allow the move. Restructuring of visitation usually involves scheduling more visitation in the summer and over other holiday breaks. In some cases, the noncustodial parent and child may actually spend more time together each year under the restructured schedule than under the original schedule, although the restructured schedule may provide for less-frequent visitation. If the court believes that frequency of contact is more important than extended periods of contact, the move is less likely to be allowed. If the parents cannot afford long-distance visits, the court is less likely to allow relocation. If visitation is affordable, the court might reduce child support to facilitate visits, or the court might assess the cost of travel on the parent who seeks to move.

If parents have joint physical custody and a child spends a substantial amount of time with both parents, a court may treat the request to move like an original custody determination. The court will try to decide which parent will best meet the child's needs. The court will consider the above factors, along with other factors usually considered in custody cases, including the child's attachment to his or her current home, school, and community.

RIGHTS OF GRANDPARENTS

In 2000, the U.S. Supreme Court issued a ruling that makes it more difficult for grandparents to obtain court-ordered visits with their grandchildren. In the case of *Troxel v. Granville*, Justice Sandra Day O'Connor, writing for a divided Court, held:

> [S]o long as a parent adequately cares for his or her child (*i.e.,* is fit), there will normally be no reason for the State to inject itself into the private realm of the family to further question the ability of that parent to make the best decisions concerning the rearing of that parent's children.

In *Troxel* the parents of the father sought visitation with their grandchildren following the death by suicide of the father.

The mother was willing to let the grandparents have time with the grandchildren during daytime hours one day per month. The grandparents wanted weekend overnight visitation twice a month. When the grandparents did not receive the visitation they wanted, they filed suit under a Washington state law that allowed "any person" to seek visitation at "any time." The U.S. Supreme Court found that the law was "breathtakingly broad" and did not give sufficient weight to the parent's desires regarding how to raise her children. The Court also found that the trial judge did not give adequate reasons for granting visitation. Thus, the Supreme Court held that granting visitation to the grandparents in this case "violated [the mother's] due process right to make decisions concerning the care, custody, and control of her daughters."

The scope of the Supreme Court's decision is uncertain. The Court certainly believed that parents should be given more deference in deciding who can associate with their children than Washington state allowed. The Court, however, left open the possibility that some grandparents would be entitled to obtain court-ordered visitation. Such visitation might be allowed, for example, if grandparents can show that they had a particularly strong relationship with their grandchildren—as, perhaps, if the grandparents had raised the grandchildren for a number of years before primary custody of the children returned to the parents.

At the time *Troxel* was decided, statutes in all states gave grandparents a right to visit with their grandchildren. The scope of that right varied from state to state. The typical statute allowed grandparents to seek an order of visitation following the separation or divorce of the parents or the death of a parent. After *Troxel,* many state legislatures have modified their grandparent visitation laws to continue allowing grandparent visitation, but with an increased burden of proof on grandparents who seek that visitation.

Generally, an order of visitation for grandparents will not be necessary if grandparents are able to see their grandchildren when the children are with the parent to whom the grandparent is related. If, however, such contact is not feasible because the parent does not regularly exercise visitation, then specific visitation for the grandparents may be ordered in appropriate circumstances.

It is possible for grandparents to obtain custody of grandchildren. If the parents consent to custody by the grandparents, the grandparents may have custody on an informal basis. Grandparents may seek to formalize the arrangement by going to court to be named guardians of their grandchildren. Some school districts may require that a grandparent be named guardian of a child before the grandparent may enroll the grandchild in school.

If grandparents seek custody of a grandchild over the parents' objection, the grandparents usually will have to show that the parents are unfit—which requires a heavy burden of proof. If, however, the grandparents have been raising their grandchild for a considerable length of time under an informal arrangement, the grandparents may have become the "psychological parents" of the grandchildren by the time the parent or parents seek to regain custody. In these circumstances, courts in many states may allow the grandparents to retain custody, even if the parents are fit.

RIGHTS AND DUTIES OF STEPPARENTS

The responsibilities of a stepparent depend on state law. A stepparent usually is not liable for the support of a spouse's child from a prior marriage, unless the stepparent has adopted the child. Absent an adoption, the child's biological parents are liable for the child's support. Some states, however, make stepparents liable for the stepchild's support as long as the stepparent and stepchild are living together.

A stepparent who does not adopt a spouse's child normally may not claim custody of the child if the marriage ends in divorce, although some states allow a stepparent to seek visitation.

A stepchild usually does not share in the estate of a stepparent, unless the stepparent has provided for the stepchild in a will. However, an unmarried stepchild under eighteen may receive survivor, retirement, or disability benefits through a stepparent's Social Security account if the stepchild was financially dependent on the stepparent.

THE WORLD AT YOUR FINGERTIPS

• For more information about the law of child custody, including information in a question-and-answer format, visit the Nolo website at *www.nolo.com*. Click on "Family Law & Immigration" to find more information about child custody and visitation.

• The FreeAdvice website also provides more detailed information about child custody, in question-and-answer format, at *http://familylaw.freeadvice.com/child_custody.*

REMEMBER THIS

• The automatic preference for granting custody to a child's mother—provided only that the mother is minimally fit—has been abolished. As a matter of law, fathers and mothers are supposed to be treated equally, although individual judges may sometimes be biased toward one parent or the other. Courts consider many factors when deciding custody, including: whether one parent or both parents have handled the day-to-day raising of the child; the amount of time the parents will have to spend with the child; the mental health of the parties; the special needs of the child; the preference of the child; and conduct by the parents that may have been harmful to the child.

• Joint custody, also known as "shared parenting," is a common option. Parenting time or visitation with a child will not be restricted unless it can be shown that the child will be harmed by a normal amount of parenting time or visitation.

• The U.S. Supreme Court has held that most court-ordered visitation for grandparents violates the parents' rights to raise their children as they see fit. However, visitation for grandparents still may be possible in exceptional circumstances, such as when the grandparents have raised the children for a significant period of time prior to the children returning to their parents' custody.

CHAPTER 14
Domestic Violence

Robin and Earl have been married for two years. Earl grew up in a home in which he was beaten by both parents. Although Earl sometimes can be very affectionate and charming, he also has periods of extreme anger. Earl regularly kicks the family's dog and cat, and has struck Robin twice, leaving bruises. Earl tries to keep Robin from seeing her parents and sisters, and he recently has accused her of having affairs (which she is not doing). What laws and services are available to protect Robin?

According to the Justice Department's Bureau of Justice Statistics, in the United States in 2001 there were 691,710 reported acts of nonfatal domestic violence—also referred to as **intimate-partner violence**. These acts of violence included assaults, rapes, and robberies. About 85 percent of the acts were committed against women, and 15 percent were committed against men.

The Justice Department also reported that in 2000, 1,247 women and 440 men were killed by intimate partners. Between 1993 and 2001, rates of intimate violence dropped significantly: a 49-percent drop in violence against females and a 42-percent drop in violence against males. There was a similar decrease in the overall rate of violent crime during the same time period.

Domestic violence occurs in all socioeconomic groups, but its incidence correlates with income. Women with family incomes under $7,500 experience the highest rates of violence: twenty out of every thousand women are abused. This rate is approximately seven times higher than the rate for women with family incomes over $75,000: only three out of every thousand are abused. In a related statistic, females residing in rental housing are three times more likely to be victims of domestic violence than females residing in owned housing.

Black females experience more domestic violence than white females: eleven out of every thousand black women are abused,

WARNING SIGNS OF DOMESTIC VIOLENCE

A person may be more likely to commit domestic violence if he or she:

- Has exhibited prior violent or threatening behavior toward family and friends

- Is easily prone to anger—for example, if he or she hits walls or drives dangerously

- Is very controlling, and tries to make all decisions

- Attempts to isolate his or her partner by keeping the partner from seeing friends and family

- Blames others for his or her own mistakes

- Is very moody—in other words, can switch quickly from being nice to being enraged

- Calls his or her partner names—for example, "stupid," "bitch," or other expletives

- Is extremely jealous, and frequently accuses his or her partner of being unfaithful

- Is cruel to animals

- Abuses drugs or alcohol

- Is experiencing economic hardship or prolonged unemployment

- Was (or is) abused by his or her own parents, or witnessed abuse of others as a child

Sources: National Center for Injury Prevention and Control; Turning Point Services; Health First; ABA Commission on Domestic Violence

TALKING TO A LAWYER

Q. *I've heard there are many more physical and mental effects of domestic violence than one might expect. Is this true?*

A. Yes. In addition to death and bodily injury, domestic violence can have many other consequences. Studies report that women with a history of intimate-partner violence have 60 percent more health problems than women with no history of abuse. Common problems include heart and circulatory problems, sexually transmitted diseases, depression, alcohol abuse, and suicide.

Battered women may lose their jobs because of absenteeism resulting from injury or illness, or taking time off from work to attend court. Battered women also may move frequently to avoid their abusers or because of economic difficulties. This may further interfere with continuity of employment and economic stability.

Children who come from families with domestic violence—whether directed at partners or at children—are more likely to be at risk for academic failure, dropping out of school, substance abuse, mental health problems, and delinquency. Boys who saw their fathers abuse their mothers are substantially more likely to be abusive in their own adult intimate relationships, as well as more violent in general.

In a 2003 report, the U.S. Centers for Disease Control and Prevention revealed that the costs of medical and mental-health care associated with intimate-partner violence against women exceeds $5.8 billion per year, and the direct economic costs of lost productivity are nearly $1.8 billion per year.

Answer by Professor Jeff Atkinson,
DePaul University College of Law, Chicago, Illinois

versus eight out of every thousand white women. The domestic violence rates between Hispanic persons and non-Hispanic persons were about the same. The highest rates of intimate violence occur in the sixteen to twenty-four age range.

Earlier Justice Department studies reported that one in four incidents of domestic violence involved an offender who had been drinking—and of those offenders who were sent to prison, about half had been drinking for six or more hours before the violence occurred.

STATE LAWS

In the last twenty-five years, state legislatures and courts have been paying increasing attention to domestic violence. Most states have laws designed to protect individuals from domestic violence by their spouses, other family members, and people with whom the victim may have had a social relationship.

A common remedy is for a court to issue an **order of protection**—also known as a **protective order**—that orders the alleged abuser to stop abusing or harassing the victim. In addition, such orders often direct the abuser to stay away from the victim and the victim's home or place of work. If the abuser continues to abuse the person protected by the order, he or she can be charged with a criminal violation of the order, as well as with other offenses such as assault and battery. Penalties include fines and incarceration.

The domestic-violence statutes in most states apply not only to physical attacks, but also to other types of conduct. Some examples of conduct that could be considered domestic violence include: creating a disturbance at a spouse's place of work, harassing telephone calls, stalking, surveillance, and threats against a spouse or family member, even if the threat is not carried out.

Studies have shown that issuing a protective order or arresting a person who commits an act of domestic violence does reduce future incidents of domestic violence. When perpetrators of domestic violence see that the police and court system will

TALKING TO A LAWYER

Q. If I obtain an order of protection, but the police fail to enforce the order, and my children or I are injured as a result, can I sue for monetary damages under federal law?

A. Probably not. In 2005, the U.S. Supreme Court decided the case of *Castle Rock v. Gonzales.* In *Gonzales,* a mother obtained a restraining order in connection with a divorce that prohibited the father from being within 100 yards of the family home, although the father was permitted to spend time with his three daughters—ages seven, nine, and ten—on alternate weekends and at a weeknight dinner. On a June evening at about 5:00 P.M., without any advance arrangements, the father picked up the three girls while they were playing outside the family home. The mother called the police and asked that the police enforce the restraining order and return the children to her immediately. The police said there was nothing they could do, and told her to call back at 10:00 P.M. if the children had not been returned. According to the mother's lawsuit, the children still were not home at 10:00 P.M. She called the police again and was told to wait until midnight to see if the father would return the children. The children never came home. The father came to the police station at 3:20 A.M. with a semiautomatic handgun. He opened fire, and was killed by the police. Inside the cab of the father's pickup truck, police found the bodies of the three girls, whom the father already had murdered.

The mother filed a civil-rights lawsuit (a section 1983 action), claiming that she had "a protected property interest" under the Fourteenth Amendment to the U.S. Constitution to have the order enforced.

A majority of the Supreme Court disagreed. The Court said it is "common sense that *all* police officers must use some discretion in deciding when and where to enforce city ordinances [or state laws]" (Court's emphasis). The Court said this was particularly true when the whereabouts of the offender are not known. Thus, although the Court expressed sympathy regarding "[t]he horrible facts of this case," the

Court did not find that the mother had a specific right to police enforcement under the federal Constitution. The Court said that although framers of the Constitution and the federal civil-rights law "did not create a system by which police departments are generally held financially accountable for crimes that better policing might have prevented," state lawmakers could create such a system if they wished.

Answer by Professor Jeff Atkinson,
DePaul University College of Law, Chicago, Illinois

treat domestic violence seriously, many such perpetrators may be deterred from future violence.

Nonetheless, studies also report that a woman who flees her abuser is at 75 percent higher risk of being murdered by that abuser than a woman who stays with the abuser. Thus, careful safety planning is essential.

Orders of protection are not guarantees of protection or safety. For some individuals with intense anger or rage, no court order will stop their violence, and a court order might even add to the rage. Each year, there are reports of women murdered by their husbands or boyfriends despite numerous arrests and orders of protection. The legal system cannot offer perfect protection, although it can reduce violence.

Many states have **victim compensation funds** that can help victims of domestic violence as well as the victims of other crimes. Such funds may cover medical costs and mental-health counseling, and provide compensation for loss of wages or support.

FEDERAL LAW

In the 2000 case *United States v. Morrison*, the Supreme Court struck down a portion of the **Violence Against Women Act**— the more formal title of which is the **Civil Rights Remedies for Gender-Motivated Violence Act**. The act had allowed a person to sue for damages if another person "commits a crime of violence motivated by gender."

The Supreme Court, although sympathetic to issues of domestic violence, held that domestic violence did not involve a sufficient connection to economic activity to be justified under the commerce clause of the U.S. Constitution. It also held that, since the conduct the act sought to prevent was private conduct rather than conduct of a state government, the act was not a proper exercise of power under the Constitution's Fourteenth Amendment.

Although the Court held that Congress did not have the power to create a private remedy for domestic violence, victims of domestic violence can still use state laws to prevent further violence and collect damages for violent acts already committed.

WHERE TO TURN FOR HELP

In a crisis situation, a call to the police is a good place to start. Many people complain that the police do not take accusations of domestic violence seriously. This may be true in some circumstances. But on the whole, police treat domestic-violence situations seriously, and police officers are receiving increased training on the subject.

The local state's attorney or district attorney may also be able to offer some help. An increasing number of hospitals, crisis intervention programs, domestic-violence shelters, and social-service agencies have programs designed to help victims of domestic violence. Agencies offering help in cases of domestic

 A NOTE OF CAUTION

Persons who commit acts of domestic violence may also closely monitor a partner's activities, including computer use and telephone calls. Victims of domestic violence should try to use a telephone or computer in a secure location, and should be aware that it is possible for an abuser to examine computer records to determine the websites a person has visited.

violence can be found in the yellow pages or online under "Domestic Violence Help," "Human Services Organizations," or "Crisis Intervention."

If you are working with an attorney in connection with a divorce, the attorney should also be able to initiate appropriate legal proceedings.

THE WORLD AT YOUR FINGERTIPS

- For a domestic violence hotline service and for more information about issues of domestic violence, call the National Domestic Violence Hotline at 1-800-799-7233, or visit *www.ndvh.org*.
- The U.S. Department of Justice offers information about domestic violence and referral sources on its website: *www.usdoj.gov/domesticviolence.htm*.
- For a list of suggestions for victims of domestic violence, visit the website of the Prosecuting Attorney of Clark County, Indiana: *www.clarkprosecutor.org/html/domviol/domvic.htm*.
- The website of the American Bar Association Commission on Domestic Violence provides information for victims of domestic violence and resource information for every state at *www.abanet.org/domviol*.
- The U.S. government's National Center for Injury Prevention and Control also provides a wide range of information about the types, incidence, risk factors, consequences, and prevention of domestic violence: *www.cdc.gov/ncipc/factsheets/ipvoverview.htm*.

REMEMBER THIS

- Most acts of domestic violence are committed against women, although 15 percent of nonfatal violent acts by intimate partners are committed against men, and 26 percent of intimate-partner murder victims are men.
- The main legal protections for victims of domestic violence are orders of protection and criminal prosecution of the offenders.

CHAPTER 15

Working With an Attorney

Tim and Courtney have been married for eight years. They live in a rental apartment and have one child. They each work outside the home and earn $40,000 per year. They have decided to divorce, but their breakup is comparatively amicable. They agree between themselves about how to divide their property and debts. With the help of a court-affiliated mediator, they have agreed to a joint-custody arrangement with their child. Do Courtney or Tim need a lawyer to handle the divorce?

When faced with a legal problem, the first question many people ask is: "Do I need to hire an attorney?" As you can probably guess, the answer is: "It depends." The need for an attorney varies with the specifics of each situation. Many factors should be considered, including:

• **How important is the issue?** For example, in a divorce, if there is a lot of money in dispute or if custody of children is genuinely at issue, an attorney's help is probably necessary. Conversely, if the dollar amount in dispute is low and no other important matters are at issue, an attorney's help may not be necessary.

• **How well do you understand the issue?** If you have been served with a pile of legal papers from someone who is suing you, and you don't understand what the papers mean or what you should do next, you should consult an attorney. If you do understand the legal issues and the steps you need to take, you may not need an attorney.

• **How emotionally involved are you, and how much negotiation is necessary?** An old adage states, "A person who represents himself has a fool for a client." Much of the time—indeed, maybe most of the time—the adage is correct. But some people are good at representing themselves. A key issue in deciding whether to represent yourself is your level of emotional involvement and your ability to assume a detached view of the controversy. If you are very angry at the other party—as in the case of a bitterly contested divorce or adoption—it may be best to have independent legal help to present the case in an organized, professional way. On the other hand, if you can keep a lid on your emotions and present logical arguments in negotiations or in court, then you may be able to represent yourself effectively.

• **How user-friendly is the court system?** Some court systems are set up to help people handle their own legal disputes. The court may have forms with clear explanations to help people initiate or respond to legal actions. Clerks and judges might be willing to tell people step-by-step what they need to do and what their rights are. Other court systems operate in the opposite fashion, or somewhere in between. Procedures may be complex and difficult for even lawyers to follow. Clerks and judges may seem to go out of their way to make things difficult for litigants. To get a sense of the extent to which a particular court system accommodates people who represent themselves, visit the courthouse or call the clerk of court with some polite questions. You also might ask friends about their experiences with the local court—assuming they have had issues similar to yours.

• **How much does legal representation cost?** Of course, an important factor in deciding whether to represent yourself is the cost of legal representation. For some, full-scale legal representation may not seem affordable. When involved in any legal dispute, you will need to perform a cost-benefit analysis and ask: "Is pursuit of this case—or some issue in the case—sufficiently important to be worth the money, time, and emotional energy?" If the stakes are high, full-scale representation may be worth the money, and may even save dollars or something else of great value. If the stakes are low, however, legal representation may not be cost-effective. You will need to calibrate the level of representation to the importance of the issue and the resources you have available to pursue the matter. This may mean full-scale representation, representation for a limited purpose, or no representation at all. (Limited-purpose representation will be discussed further at the end of this section.)

EXAMPLES OF WHEN LEGAL REPRESENTATION IS NECESSARY . . . OR NOT

A man and woman have been married for two years. They have no children. They both work and are capable of self-support. They decide their marriage was a mistake. Although they each harbor some anger toward the other over the failed marriage, they are able to agree on how to divide their property. (Each will keep what they brought into the marriage, and they will divide approximately equally a joint money market account after paying off their MasterCard debt.)

If the main goal of each person is to end the marriage and go their separate ways, and neither wants financial support from the other, neither the man nor the woman may need a lawyer. If the court system is user-friendly, they may be able to process their own divorce. If the court system is complicated, or if they do not want to be bothered with learning how to do the paperwork, one of them may hire a lawyer to process the divorce and the other can choose to be unrepresented and consent to the terms of the divorce. If the unrepresented party becomes uneasy about his or her rights or about the fairness of the agreement, that party should seek legal advice.

Another example: A woman and man have been married for twenty years. They have three children, ages nine to sixteen. The husband owns his own business—a chain of snack shops. The wife stayed home to take care of the children for eight years, and has worked part-time since then. The husband wants a divorce. The wife does not, but realizes that divorce seems inevitable. They dispute many issues, including the value of the husband's business, the disposition of the home, the wife's request for alimony, and the amount of child support.

In this case, both the wife and husband need representation. There are many financial issues to sort out. Expert advice probably will be necessary to determine the value of the business, division of property, and support for the wife and children. If the wife does not trust the husband's financial statements, she has all the more reason to obtain legal help. If

one party seeks a portion of a retirement or profit-sharing plan established by the other, a lawyer's services will be necessary to draw up the
appropriate papers for dividing the parties' interests and avoiding adverse tax consequences.

A final example: A husband and wife, both thirty-five, dispute custody of
their children, ages five and seven. Both want sole custody. Both have
been actively involved in raising the children.

The husband and wife will need representation if the issue of custody
will be contested in court. The emotional issue of custody is usually too
sensitive for parents to be able to represent themselves. Before going to
court, however, the parties may wish to see if they can settle their dispute through use of a mediator. A mediator is usually a mental-health professional or a lawyer who will work with the parties to attempt to reach
a solution that is acceptable to them and in the best interest of their children. (The next chapter will discuss mediation and other alternative
means of dispute resolution.)

When seeking legal help, or when considering whether or
not to represent yourself, keep in mind that it is not always necessary to hire a lawyer for full-scale representation. You can hire
a lawyer for a limited purpose. For example, at the beginning or
in the middle of a dispute, you can hire a lawyer simply to give
advice or review a document. You can pay a lawyer for one to
three hours of consultations in which you explain the facts of
your case and seek the lawyer's advice about your rights, additional steps you will need to take, and the likely outcome of the
case. You then can tailor your plans for handling the case based
on the perspectives gained from the lawyer. Using a lawyer for a
limited purpose rather than full representation sometimes is referred to as **unbundling** legal services.

You can also hire a lawyer for the purpose of negotiating a
settlement, without committing to hire the lawyer for a long, expensive trial. Alternative dispute resolution strategies—including
mediation, arbitration, and collaborative law, will be discussed in
Chapter 16.

Even if you already have a lawyer, you may want to consider hiring another lawyer—not for full representation, but to provide a second opinion. Just as patients often want a second opinion before undertaking major medical treatment, it can be prudent to seek a second legal opinion before taking a major legal action that could impact your life for years to come.

FINDING A LAWYER

Just as there are specialists in medicine, there are specialists in law. Some lawyers practice exclusively or primarily in family law. The need for a specialist will vary based on the facts of your case. If you are dealing with complex issues of property or custody, it is probably best to seek a lawyer with substantial experience in family law. If you want to adopt a child to whom you are not related, it is best to work with a lawyer with significant experience in the area of adoption, particularly if the adoption involves a child from another country or if the adoption is arranged privately rather than through an agency.

If you are adopting a child who is already in your family, and if no one is contesting the adoption, the procedure is more rou-

 THE COST OF A SPECIALIST

Hiring a specialist in family law does not necessarily cost more than hiring an attorney in general practice. However, if you are seeking an attorney with a very good reputation in any field, the fees are likely to be higher than the fees for less-prominent attorneys. Keep in mind that using a specialist can sometimes save money, to the extent that the specialist knows an area of law very well and can handle a case more efficiently than a nonspecialist.

tine and could probably be handled by a nonspecialist. For example, if an aunt and uncle wish to adopt a nephew following death of his parents, or if a stepfather is adopting his stepchild without opposition from the biological father, the process should be quick and simple. (It might even be completed by the adoptive parents themselves without the need for an attorney.)

Finding a Specialist

As of 2005, approximately eight states or state bar associations certify attorneys as specialists in family law. The requirements for certification of specialists vary from state to state, but usually certification requires several years of experience in the area of specialty and demonstration of knowledge in that area, such as through an examination (beyond the basic bar examination required of lawyers in most states). The eight states that certify specialists in family law or domestic relations are: Arizona, California, Florida, Louisiana, Minnesota, New Mexico, North Carolina, and Texas.

In states that do not officially certify specialists, lawyers still specialize—they just are not officially recognized as specialists by a state licensing agency or bar association. (In many states, lawyers may advertise that they have been certified by a private organization.)

The **American Academy of Matrimonial Lawyers,** a national organization, also certifies family law specialists. The academy is a private organization with more than 1,500 members. In order to become a member of the academy, a lawyer must have devoted 75 percent or more of his or her practice to family law for a period of at least ten years. Written or oral examinations are required, along with recommendations from judges and other lawyers. Membership in the academy does not automatically guarantee that a lawyer is highly skilled, but it does guarantee that a lawyer has substantial experience in family law. (For information about how to contact the academy, see the "World at Your Fingertips" section at the end of this chapter.)

Referrals

State, county, and city bar associations usually make referrals to lawyers. However, bar associations vary in the degree to which they screen these lawyers. Some bar associations will make referrals to all lawyers who declare themselves available to practice in a particular field. Other bar associations may require lawyers to submit proof of their experience in the relevant area. When calling a bar association's general telephone number, ask for the association's lawyer referral service.

If you are looking for a lawyer and you are low on funds, a possible source of help is a law school's legal clinic. Legal clinics will sometimes take family law cases at no charge or for a low charge. Clinics are staffed by law students working under the supervision of professors and attorneys. If the law school clinic is not able to take your case, the clinic may be able to refer you to other low-cost legal services.

Legal Assistance Foundations (LAFs) have also been established in some areas. LAFs are not-for-profit organizations that offer free or discounted legal help in civil cases, including family law cases.

Other sources of referrals to lawyers working in family law include the yellow pages, newspaper ads, and the Internet. As is

 QUALITY OF LAWYERING

Quality of lawyering is not necessarily proportional to the size or stylishness of an advertisement. If an advertisement proudly proclaims that a lawyer handles not only divorces, but also drunk-driving cases, wills, personal-injury claims, employment disputes, real estate, bankruptcy, and incorporation, the client most likely will be dealing with a generalist rather than a specialist. The lawyer also may prefer high-volume, quickly handled cases to complicated, time-intensive cases. As noted before, this approach can be fine for some cases, but not for others.

true of any advertising, however, the phrase "Let the buyer beware" always applies.

Friends and colleagues (including lawyers who work in areas other than family law) may also be able to recommend a lawyer. If a friend is basing a recommendation on personal experience, try to find out more about the friend's case and how similar it is to yours: What was at issue? Property? Support? Custody? How complicated was the case? How diligent and approachable was the lawyer?

Within the area of family law, lawyers also may specialize or have areas in which they perform particularly well (or not so well). Some lawyers are masterful at finding hidden assets and dealing with complex financial issues, but those same lawyers may not be as skilled at handling the intense emotions and more subjective issues involved in custody cases. Some lawyers are good at both. When talking with a lawyer, try to get a sense of the lawyer's experience and the extent to which he or she enjoys handling the types of issues that are relevant to your case.

FEES AND COSTS

Lawyer's Fees

Lawyer's fees will vary depending on a lawyer's locale and level of experience. The more experience, expertise, and skill a lawyer has, the higher the fee—usually, though not always. Lawyers in urban areas generally charge more than lawyers in rural areas, with the rates of suburban lawyers generally falling somewhere in between.

Most family lawyers charge on an hourly basis. A lawyer's total fee will be equal to the total hours he or she spent working on the case, multiplied by the lawyer's hourly rate. Different lawyers within a firm may have different hourly rates. Some lawyers charge different rates for appearing in court and for working in their offices. The courtroom rate may be higher on the assumption that working in court involves extra skills and pressure. Other lawyers view their office skills and courtroom skills as equally valuable, and thus charge the same rate for both types of service.

Time spent in court is not the only time a lawyer bills to a client. Lawyers may spend a significant amount of time in their offices reviewing documents, conducting research, planning strategy, talking to witnesses, talking to opposing counsel, drafting letters, and preparing papers for filing in court.

If other lawyers in the office or **paralegals** spend time on the case, their time usually will be billed as well. A paralegal is a person with specialized legal training who, although not a lawyer, assists the lawyer with legal tasks. Under a lawyer's supervision, a paralegal may do many of the same things a lawyer does, though in most states a paralegal may not represent a client in court.

A lawyer's secretary also helps the lawyer handle cases, but in most offices the secretary's time is not billed separately. In some offices, if a secretary must work overtime because a case is on an expedited schedule or is unusually demanding, the secretary's time might be billed separately.

Costs

In addition to fees for the lawyer's (and paralegal's) services, clients also usually pay **costs**. Costs are the out-of-pocket expenses associated with a case, including:

- **Court filing fees**—fees paid to the court by a person who files or responds to a lawsuit;
- **Process server fees**—fees paid to the person who delivers papers to the opposing party advising them that a lawsuit has been filed;
- **Subpoena fees**—fees paid to persons who must appear in court or deliver documents to a party, perhaps including travel costs;
- **Court reporter fees**—fees paid to court employees or private services to record court proceedings or depositions and pre-

pare a written transcript of what took place. (A **deposition** is a procedure in which an attorney prepares for a possible trial by asking questions of a party or witness under oath.)

- **Expert's fees**—fees paid to experts who testify or otherwise provide expertise or assistance in a case—for example, fees to an accountant to ascertain the value of a business or pension plan, or fees to a psychiatrist or psychologist to conduct a custody evaluation.
- **Photocopying and telephone expenses**—particularly if there is a large quantity of photocopying, long-distance phone calls, or faxes; and
- **Travel expenses**—if the attorney must travel out of town in connection with the case.

Fixed Fees

Although most attorneys charge hourly rates, some charge a fixed fee for handling an entire case. Many attorneys advertise low fixed fees—often in the range of $400 to $1,000—for handling a "simple divorce." However, such rates usually will apply only if a case is *very* simple—in other words, if virtually nothing is contested and the paperwork is routine. If a case becomes more complicated, expect higher fees. If a lawyer is not willing to enter into a fixed-fee arrangement, you should ask the attorney about the range of possible fees and costs and the factors that will make those fees higher or lower.

Many lawyers are reluctant to commit to fixed fees, since it can be difficult to predict the amount of effort necessary to handle a case at the beginning—particularly if it is uncertain how many issues will be in dispute and how contentious the opposing side will be. In addition, use of an hourly rather than a fixed fee can help an attorney control the client's demands and limit expenses that are not cost-effective. For example, if a client sees that fees are mounting, he or she will be less likely to telephone the attorney or insist that the attorney expend substantial efforts over minor details.

Other Fee Arrangements

Attorneys in family law cases typically charge a **retainer** or an **advance on fees**. In effect, a retainer is a down payment on the attorney's fees and costs. In some cases, the attorney may seek the entire fee up-front. If a case is eventually handled for an amount less than that of the retainer or advance, the attorney should return the unused portion of the fee.

Lawyers also may require a **refresh** arrangement, in which the client agrees to maintain a credit balance in his or her account with the lawyer. When the credit balance drops below a certain amount—say, $1,000 or $5,000—the client will be obliged to provide more funds. This arrangement is somewhat similar to having a security deposit with a landlord. In part, it serves as a guarantee that the final payment will be made. Many lawyers accept credit card payments, and the fee agreement with the client may provide that charges will be processed automatically through the credit card if the balance drops below a certain amount.

Contingency fees, like those used by attorneys who handle personal-injury cases, are generally prohibited in family law cases. With a contingency fee, an attorney collects a fee only if a particular result is achieved—or, alternatively, the attorney may collect a portion of whatever monetary award is received by the client. However, courts do not want to give attorneys a vested interest in facilitating divorce. For example, suppose a client wishes to reconcile with his spouse, but his attorney arranges to receive a portion of whatever property award the client receives in a divorce settlement. In this situation, the attorney may have an incentive to oppose what is best for his client, because he stands to profit from the divorce his client does not want.

Because courts wish to avoid these types of situations, contingency fees are generally prohibited in family law cases. An exception will be made in some states if the amount of money due to a client is fixed. If, for example, a client is owed a fixed amount in *past-due* child support or alimony, an attorney might be able to charge a contingency fee to collect the past-due support, since the likelihood of a conflict of interest related to the client's possible reconciliation is minimal.

Fee Agreements

If you hire an attorney for representation beyond a consultation, he or she likely will present you with a written **fee agreement** stating the services covered, the cost of those services, and the times at which payment will be due. You may choose to sign the agreement when it is presented, but it is quite permissible for you to take the agreement home, read it over, and think about it before deciding whether to sign. You should always read the agreement carefully and ask the attorney any questions you may have about the agreement.

In divorce cases, courts usually have the power to order one party to pay the other party's attorney's fees if there is a substantial difference in the income or property of the parties. If, for example, the husband earns a great deal more than the wife, the husband may be ordered to pay all or a portion of the wife's attorney's fees. If both parties have similar earning capacities or if both parties receive ample amounts of liquid assets as part of the divorce, the husband and wife are more likely to pay their own fees.

One party might also have to pay the other party's legal fees if he or she has shown **bad faith** towards the other party. For example, if you engage in misconduct or do something you should not have done—such as not paying child support or interfering with the other party's access to a child—then you likely will have to pay the fees of the other party. In addition, if you make legal or factual arguments that are **frivolous,** meaning without legal merit, then you or your attorney may be required to pay the legal fees incurred by the other party in responding to those arguments.

An order that one party must pay the other party's fees is not a license for the other party to accumulate any amount of fees that he or she wishes; the fees must be reasonable. A court can look at the facts of the case and decide what constitutes a reasonable fee for the issue before the court.

TALKING TO A LAWYER

Q. If I think a bill from my lawyer is too high, what should I do?

A. You should start by talking to your lawyer and explaining your concerns. If the two of you cannot resolve the issue by yourselves, in most states you can use the services of a fee-arbitration program. If that option is unavailable or fails to produce a resolution, you can simply refuse to pay the full amount, and wait for your lawyer to commence a legal action to recover the fee. In that lawsuit, you can argue to a judge that the lawyer's fee was unreasonable.

Answer by Professor Barbara Atwood,
Mary Anne Richey Professor of Law
at the University of Arizona, Tucson, Arizona

HELPING THE LAWYER HELP YOU

Well-prepared clients help their cases go more smoothly. If you are involved in a lawsuit, you can save time and money by gathering facts and carefully considering what goals you want to achieve.

For example, if property or support is contested, you can help your lawyer by gathering together your financial information. You can prepare inventories of the assets and liabilities of your marriage, itemizing the value or cost of each significant item, if known. Statements of the parties' incomes and expenses also are usually necessary. You can find this kind of financial information in copies of tax returns, checking account records, investment account records, and charge account records. If you do not know certain information, you can make lists of what is known, what is not known, and where more information might be located.

If you or your ex have been divorced before, you should try to obtain copies of the earlier divorce papers—particularly the marital settlement agreement and final order of the court.

DOCUMENTS TO ASSEMBLE

To help your lawyer analyze your case and provide better advice, it may be useful for you to assemble all of the relevant documents relating to your marriage. Such documents may include:

- Tax returns (state and federal) for the last three years, and perhaps for earlier years as well

- Records of bank accounts—checking, saving, money market—and certificates of deposit

- Investment account records

- Statements from pension plans or profit-sharing plans

- Recent pay stubs for yourself and your spouse

- Credit card statements and records pertaining to other bills and expenses

- Deeds to your home and other real estate; any leases

- Automobile titles

- A list and description of insurance policies—health, home, auto, life, and disability

- Divorce decrees and settlement agreements from earlier marriages

- Resumes or curriculum vitae

- A copy of your written premarital agreement, if there was one

- Other documents you think are relevant

If custody is at issue, you can make lists of reasons why you should have custody of your children. Your reasons should be as specific as possible. Include names, addresses, and telephone numbers of persons who might be able to testify in support of these arguments. You should also list the arguments your spouse is likely to make, and any evidence your spouse will have in support of his or her position. Divorce is a time of stress, and it probably will not be easy to methodically and logically gather information. But the information-gathering process can be therapeutic—think of it as taking steps to gain more control of your current environment and future.

Although divorce is a time of stress, it also is a time to plan for the future. You should develop short-term and long-term goals, and try to figure out how issues of property, support, and time with your children will fit in with those goals. By identifying which issues are most important and which issues are less crucial, you will help yourself and your attorney resolve your situation in an orderly way while developing a reasonable plan for the future.

Many attorneys will ask clients to fill out detailed questionnaires regarding finances and custody issues, if applicable. If your attorney asks you to fill out such a form, do so promptly. It

 PREPARING A WRITTEN NARRATIVE

Some attorneys ask their clients to write a narrative statement about their marriage and divorce. Such a statement might include descriptions of:

- significant events in the marriage,

- reasons for the divorce,

- child-raising responsibilities,

- contributions each party made to the marriage—financial, home-making, or otherwise,

- good qualities and bad qualities of each party,

- your short-term and long-term goals and the reasons behind those goals; and

- your perceptions of your spouse's short-term and long-term goals and the reasons behind them.

Creating a written narrative may prove cathartic, and may help both you and your attorney to understand the relevant issues better.

will help your attorney to organize the case and determine what information and arguments need to be developed.

In the heat of a contested divorce, it may be tempting to contact your attorney frequently to blow off steam and seek advice. In most cases, however, this will not be an effective use of the attorney's time or your money. Usually it is best to save up a batch of inquiries and then discuss them with the attorney in a single sitting. Of course, if something urgent arises—such as the other party changing the residence of the children or hiding major assets—you should notify your attorney promptly.

It helps to understand that attorneys are not always able to take your calls immediately. Attorneys are often busy with trials, meetings, or other clients. A well-organized attorney, however, will be able to return calls within twenty-four hours, or will arrange for a staff member to call you back. Often you can relay an inquiry or piece of information to the attorney's secretary or paralegal, who will then discuss the matter with the attorney and call you back.

It is important for you to be honest with your attorney. If there are skeletons in your closet (or a few loose bones) regarding finances, extramarital relationships, or other issues, it is best to be candid about such matters so they can be dealt with as necessary. A client usually is worse off if adverse information surfaces for the first time in the middle of a trial or negotiation, since the attorney may not be fully prepared to respond to such information.

Family law attorneys hear many secrets about people's private lives. An attorney is not likely to be shocked or upset by any disclosures you make. Under rules of confidentiality, an attorney must keep a client's secrets—even if a client reveals that he or she did something illegal in the past. However, an attorney cannot help a client pursue present or future illegal conduct. If the attorney has given information to the court or opposing side that the attorney later learns to be false, he or she usually is obliged to correct the information.

In a bitter divorce, it is common for clients to want their at-

DANGER OF DISPLAYING ANGER IN COURT

In contested cases, parties often are angry at each other. This is understandable. But displays of anger—particularly in court—usually are counterproductive.

In one case, for example, a joint-custody arrangement allowed for a child to spend approximately equal time with both parents. However, the arrangement was not working out, and both the mother and father sought to modify custody. The court ordered the parties to attend counseling sessions, but the father would not attend because he refused to communicate directly with the mother. At the end of the case, the trial judge described the father's conduct in court as follows:

> During [the father's] testimony he was visibly angry and his body language appeared to show a strong disliking for [the mother]. To this extent Father exhibited a lack of control of his negative feelings for Mother in the presence of the Court. The same or worse is likely outside the courtroom in the company of Mother and/or the children.

For this and other reasons, the court granted sole custody to the mother, and the Idaho Supreme Court affirmed the decision.

Source: McGriff v. McGriff (*Idaho 2004*).

torneys to act as avenging angels—to make life miserable for their spouse and their spouse's attorney. However, this is not the proper function of an attorney. An attorney's job is to give calm, reasonable advice and to pursue a case in a diligent manner. Diligence and competence do not require antagonism or treating opposing counsel or parties with disrespect.

An attorney who yells and screams is usually out of control and not serving the client's interest. The system of justice works better, and cases generally turn out better, when attorneys deal with each other (and with the court) in a civil manner.

THE WORLD AT YOUR FINGERTIPS

• The American Bar Association's lawyer referral service provides online links and other information about lawyer referral services in different parts of the country. Visit *www.abanet.org/legalservices/lris/directory.html#.*

• For state-by-state information about certification of attorneys specializing in family law, visit the website of the American Bar Association Standing Committee on Specialization at *www.abanet.org/legalservices/specialization/statestatus.html.*

• The American Academy of Matrimonial Lawyers can be reached at 150 N. Michigan Avenue, Suite 2040, Chicago, Illinois 60601; by telephone at 312-263-6477; and on the Web at *www.aaml.org.* The academy also has chapters in many states.

REMEMBER THIS

• Whether you need to hire a lawyer depends on many factors, including: (1) the importance of the issue; (2) how well you understand the issue; (3) how emotionally involved you are in the issue; (4) the degree to which the local court system is user-friendly; and (5) the cost of representation.

• You do not always need to hire a lawyer for full-scale representation. Sometimes it is helpful to hire a lawyer for a session or two of advice and perspective.

• Most lawyers charge an hourly rate, plus extra amounts for out-of-pocket costs associated with the case. If a case is simple or the amount of work is very predictable, a fixed fee may be possible. You should discuss with your lawyer the range of possible fees, the factors that will affect those fees, and the likelihood that one party may be required to pay some of the other party's fees.

CHAPTER 16

Mediation and
Other Alternatives

*Steve decided to divorce Rosalyn after Rosalyn admitted having
an affair with a coworker. Both parties are angry with each other
and seek sole custody of their children—a boy, age eight, and a
girl, age ten. Before embarking on a contested custody trial, the
court requires that the couple attempt mediation. The mediator
will try to help Steve and Rosalyn focus on what is best for the
children and devise a solution that seems best for all of them.
The mediator, however, cannot force a settlement.*

Working with lawyers and courts is not the only way of
resolving disputes. Over time, as people have grown
increasingly weary of the lengthiness, expense, and adversarial
nature of litigation, both nonlawyers and lawyers have sought
other means of solving problems. Solving problems without going
to court to have a judge decide an issue is referred to as **alternative dispute resolution** (**ADR**).

Many methods of ADR are used in conjunction with court
proceedings. For example, if a couple seeks a divorce, it may use
a mediator to help resolve issues of custody, property, and support, but the couple will still need to go to court to have a judge
enter an order officially ending the marriage.

There are several ways of resolving family law disputes, outlined below, that may help you avoid going to court altogether.

MEDIATION

Mediation is a process by which the parties to a divorce (or
some other dispute) try to resolve their disagreements outside of
court with the help of a mediator. The mediator cannot force a
settlement, but tries to help the parties clarify their interests and
devise their own solution.

In divorce proceedings, mediators are often involved in custody and parenting-time disputes. (Parenting time is time the child spends with each parent.) In some jurisdictions, particularly large urban areas, courts require mediation of custody and visitation disputes. The mother and father must talk with a court-appointed mediator to try to resolve the problem before putting their case before a judge. The mediator may also talk to the children.

Court-ordered mediation is usually provided at no cost or at low cost to the parties, though the parties must pay the filing fees required to initiate the court action.

Mediators also can handle property disputes and support disputes. However, a couple seeking mediation of disputes on financial issues probably will have to seek a private mediator, since most court-affiliated mediators deal with only issues of custody and parenting time.

If the parties resolve their disagreements through mediation, the attorneys for one or both of the parties can still be involved in finalizing and approving the agreement. Alternatively, if the parties feel comfortable working without attorneys and can get the paperwork right, they may draft their own mediated settlement as an **agreed order** and take it to a judge for approval.

Most mediators are either mental-health professionals or attorneys. Many mediators, particularly those associated with court mediation services, have degrees in social work or psychology. Private mediators—hired by the parties on their own—are often attorneys, although many are mental-health professionals.

During mediation, mediators who are mental health-professionals are not serving as therapists, and mediators who are attorneys are not serving as attorneys. Rather, they are working as professional mediators trying to help two or more people work out their differences.

Mediation often has the advantage of being cheaper and quicker than prolonged negotiations by attorneys or a contested trial before a judge. Moreover, a good mediator can help the parties build their problem-solving skills, which can help them avoid later disputes. Most people who settle their cases through mediation leave the process feeling better than if they had gone through a bitter court fight.

However, mediation also can have disadvantages—at least in certain cases. For example, if the purpose of mediation is to settle financial issues and one party is hiding assets or income, the other party might be better off with an attorney who can vigorously investigate the matter. Mediators are usually good at exploring the parties' needs, goals, and possible solutions, but unlike attorneys, they do not have the legal resources to look for hidden information—for example, they cannot subpoena documents or witnesses.

Mediation also might not work if one party is very passive and likely to be bulldozed by the other. In such a situation, the mediated agreement might be lopsided in favor of the stronger party. A good mediator, however, will see to it that a weaker party's needs are expressed and protected. Mediators may refuse to proceed with mediation if it looks as though one side will take improper advantage of the other.

Some legal and mental-health professionals think that mediation is not appropriate if a case involves domestic violence. One concern is that mediation will give the abuser an opportunity to harm the victim again. Another concern is that victims of physical abuse are not able adequately to express and protect their own interests. However, other professionals believe that disputes in families with a history of domestic violence still can be mediated, particularly if the victim does not feel significantly intimidated by the abuser at the time of mediation, or if the mediator is adept at making sure the abused party's needs are explored and met.

A final disadvantage of mediation may be that, if the mediation does not succeed, the parties may have wasted time and money on mediation and still face the expense of a trial.

There are no firm, nationwide figures regarding the percentage of cases resolved through mediation, but studies of mediated custody disputes in several large cities report that between 50 and 90 percent of such cases are resolved by mediation.

ADVISORY OPINIONS

Instead of going to a formal trial before a judge, the parties and their attorneys may submit their case to one or more experienced family law attorneys for an advisory opinion about how the case would likely be decided if it went to court. In effect, this process constitutes a mini-trial that is not binding.

When seeking an advisory opinion, the attorneys for the husband and wife submit their cases to a family law attorney. With the clients present, the attorneys for the husband and wife make oral presentations and submit documents. The amount of time allowed for this "mini-trial" is set by agreement, but one to four hours is common. After submission of "evidence," the experienced family law attorney issues an opinion and the reasons for that opinion. In many cases, the advisory opinion induces the parties to settle the case, although they still have the right to proceed to trial before a judge.

In some cities, there is an established panel of attorneys who issue advisory opinions. The attorneys may hear cases and issue opinions at no charge or at specified rates, depending on local custom. If there is no established panel of family law attorneys to issue advisory opinions, clients and their attorneys may still seek out an attorney who is willing to serve in such a capacity.

A variation on this approach is for the attorneys to talk to a judge before trial, presenting the essential facts and arguments of their cases and asking the judge for an informal opinion. The judge may then reveal to the attorneys how he or she would be likely to decide a trial based on the facts presented, and how that decision might differ if particular facts were different.

Some judges will allow clients to sit in on these meetings; others will not. The judge's decision to allow a client to sit in on such a meeting—sometimes called a **settlement conference**—may hinge on the judge's perception of whether it will help the case. Judges do not want clients to become disruptive or emotionally upset at settlement conferences. In addition, some judges

SUCCESSFUL SETTLEMENT CONFERENCES

Settlement conferences with a judge may work best when the judge who handles the settlement conference is different from the judge who will hear the trial if the case is not settled. When the judges are different, the attorneys and parties are more likely to be open and frank with the settlement conference judge about what they would be willing to settle for. Often, this can help resolve the case without a trial. If the judge handling the settlement conference will also hear the trial, the attorneys and the parties may be less inclined to be frank with the judge, out of concern that the judge will limit his future rulings based on what he knows the parties are willing to settle for.

---

are concerned that if a client hears the judge's likely opinion based on certain facts, that client will assume the judge is prejudiced. In fact, a judge's comments at a settlement conference do not mean the judge is prejudiced. Rather, such comments usually mean simply that if the parties prove a certain set of facts, a certain result can be expected. If they prove different facts, they will likely attain a different result.

ARBITRATION

Another form of alternative dispute resolution is **arbitration**. Arbitration is not widely used in family law cases, but it is an option in some states.

In arbitration, the parties agree to submit their dispute to a third party (other than a judge) for a binding decision. Often the arbitrator is an attorney or retired judge who is able to hear a case in a more expedited manner than would a court. Arbitration may be expeditious in two respects. First, the arbitrator may be able to hold a hearing in the case sooner than a trial judge, particularly if the trial judge has a calendar crowded with many cases. Second, arbitration may take less time than a trial, since arbitration procedures often are more informal and the attorneys proceed more quickly. If the arbitration proceeds more quickly than would a trial, arbitration will save time and costs. Costs of arbitration vary, but are usually similar to attorneys' hourly rates. (For further discussion of attorney's fees and costs, see Chapter 15.)

In many states, husbands and wives are allowed to arbitrate issues of property and alimony. But although most courts have neither specifically endorsed nor rejected the practice of arbitration, courts in most states are not likely to approve binding arbitration of custody and child support disputes. Courts usually view themselves as ultimately responsible for protecting a child's welfare, and courts are reluctant to yield authority to an outside arbitrator.

In one New York case, for example, a mother and father agreed to have their marital disputes settled by a three-member rabbinical court that was serving as an arbitration panel. The rabbinical court awarded joint custody to the father and mother. But the state court declined to follow the rabbinical court's decision, noting that joint custody was not in the best interest of the children because of the "extreme antagonism" between the parents. However, the state court did **confirm** (uphold) the rabbinical court's determination of maintenance.

COLLABORATIVE LAW

Collaborative law is a relatively new area of law in which people resolve their disputes without contested court hearings. Collaborative law can be applied in divorces as well as other types of disputes.

Under principles of collaborative law, the parties hire attorneys with the understanding that those attorneys can only be used to help *settle* the dispute. In the event their case does not settle, the parties agree to hire new attorneys to handle a trial. The parties and their attorneys then work together as a team to gather and share information, and to reach a settlement that they all think meets the parties' needs—or at least a settlement they can live with. Usually, collaborative law provides a comparatively peaceful and less costly way to resolve disputes than a trial. If a settlement is not reached, however, there will be added costs for hiring new attorneys and mounting a trial.

Depending on the desires of the attorneys and the parties, collaborative-law cases may utilize experts or consultants, in addition to attorneys, to help resolve the case. Such experts or consultants may include:

• "Coaches"—that is, mental-health professionals who can help the parties sort through their emotions and engage in effective negotiations;

• Financial specialists to gather information about the parties' finances, place values on property, and assist in future financial planning; and

• Child specialists, who can talk to any children involved with the case to determine their needs and help the parties develop a parenting plan.

Before entering into a collaborative-law agreement, the parties should have a reasonable amount of trust in each other and believe that the other side will work in good faith to resolve the issues without a trial. Deciding to use collaborative law is a way of demonstrating commitment to handling a case in a cooperative way. Collaborative law provides a structure that may result in an efficient settlement and development of the parties' problem-solving skills—*if* the parties are ready to negotiate in good faith.

THE WORLD AT YOUR FINGERTIPS

• For more information about mediation, visit the Divorceinfo website at *www.divorceinfo.com/mediation.htm.*

• You can find a mediator through the yellow pages (look under "Mediation"); on the Internet (search for "divorce mediation" and the name of your city or state); and perhaps through referral services run by hospitals. In addition, the local clerk of court can tell you if your court system has a mediation service.

REMEMBER THIS

• An alternative to resolving disputes through the courts is mediation. A mediator helps the parties focus on their genuine interests and resolve disputes, but the mediator cannot force a settlement. Mediation usually works well if the parties conduct themselves in good faith and one party is not trying to dominate or bulldoze the other. If mediation is successful, a court will approve the settlement, and the parties will have avoided the emotional and financial costs of a trial.

• Arbitration, although not commonly used in family law cases, is an option in some states—particularly in the case of financial issues associated with a divorce. In arbitration, the parties agree to have an arbitrator take the place of a judge. An arbitrator issues a decision that is binding on the parties. Arbitration procedures may be quicker and less costly than a trial in the courts.

CHAPTER 17

Where Do You Go From Here?

A Note from the Editors at the ABA

No matter where you are in your familial life, it's a good bet that there's a song that fits your situation. From "Chances Are" to "Just the Two of Us" to "We Are Family" to, sadly, "Breaking Up is Hard to Do" (or "50 Ways to Leave Your Lover"), there's a song out there that relates to each of us.

We've given you a great deal of information in this book, but we're not ready for our swan song just yet. Instead, we've compiled even more resources for you to check out. (A few of these may have been mentioned in previous chapters, but we still think they're the best places for you to start.)

IT'S ALL RELATIVE: NINE WEBSITES TO GET YOU STARTED

Some of these websites are housed within larger sites—but they do contain rather lengthy sections on topics associated with family law. You're bound to find what you're looking for at one of these sites, or from one of their links.

Nolo.com—*www.nolo.com* (click on "Family Law" for information on living together, marriage, divorce, child custody, and more).

The 'Lectric Law Library *Lawcopedia*'s Family Law Topic Area—*www.lectlaw.com/tfam.html*.

The American Bar Association Family Law Section—*www.abanet.org/family*.

FreeAdvice.com's Family Law section—*www.family-law. freeadvice.com*.

Family Violence Prevention Fund—*www.endabuse.org.*

FindLaw for the Public: Divorce & Family Law Center—*http://public.findlaw.com/family_law/.*

DivorceNet—*www.divorcenet.com.*

National Adoption Information Clearinghouse—*http://naic.acf.hhs.gov.*

National Council for Adoption—*www.ncfa-usa.org* (click on "Adoption Factbook III" under "Publications").

A NOVEL IDEA: READ MORE ABOUT IT

While none of these books is actually a novel, each one makes for informative and valuable reading. Remember, these are just a few picks to start with, on a variety of topics relating to family law. Don't forget to check out what your local library has to offer, in addition to Amazon.com and other online bookstores.

A Legal Guide for Lesbian and Gay Couples. Hayden Curry, Denis Clifford, Frederick Hertz. (Nolo Press, February 2004.)

Living Together: A Legal Guide for Unmarried Couples. Toni Lynne Ihara, Ralph E. Warner, Frederick Hertz. (Nolo Press, February 2004.)

The Adoption Resource Book. Lois Gilman. (HarperResource, November 1998.)

DON'T FORGET

While websites and books are great places to get information, you might also want to see if any local venues offer courses, lectures and seminars, or expert panels related to the topic of family law. Check with your local library, bar association, colleges, senior citizens' centers, and hospitals (to name just a few) to see if anything is in the works. Your local radio and TV stations may also provide some relevant programming.

And don't forget about the countless posting boards, user

groups, mailing lists, and chat rooms that exist on the Internet. Many of these could help you in your quest for knowledge and/or provide a network of support, depending on the issues you're facing. Communicating with others who have been in your position is a great way to learn about other avenues to explore, and what pitfalls to avoid.

We hope we've provided you with enough information to get you started, and we welcome your comments and suggestions for future editions of this book.

Please visit us on the Web at *www.abanet.org/publiced* or drop us a line via e-mail at abapubed@abanet.org.

INDEX

ABOUT THE AUTHOR

Jeff Atkinson is an Adjunct Professor at DePaul University College of Law in Chicago, Illinois. Professor Atkinson has taught a variety of subjects, including family law, health care law, and ethics. He also serves as a professor-reporter for the Illinois Judicial Conference, responsible for training Illinois judges in family law and legal ethics.

He is the author of a two-volume treatise entitled *Modern Child Custody Practice—Second Edition,* published by Lexis-Nexis, San Francisco, CA. He is former chair of the American Bar Association's (ABA's) Child Custody Committee, and has served as a member of the ABA's Family Law Section Council, the editorial board of the ABA's *Family Advocate,* and the editorial board of the *Family Law Quarterly.* He also serves as Chief Judge of the ABA Family Law Section's Howard Schwab Essay Contest. Professor Atkinson's writings on family law and other subjects have been cited by the United States Supreme Court and the supreme courts of eleven states.

Professor Atkinson serves as a reporter and advisor to the National Conference of Commissioners on Uniform State Laws, an organization which drafts law for the states on family law issues and other topics. Jeff Atkinson lives in Wilmette, Illinois and is a member of the Avoca District 37 School Board. He is admitted to the bars of the State of Illinois and the United States Supreme Court and has practiced law since 1977.